interchange

FOURTH EDITION

Jack C. Richards

With Jonathan Hull and Susan Proctor

Series Editor: David Bohlke

CAMBRIDGE
UNIVERSITY PRESS

STUDENT'S BOOK 1

CAMBRIDGE UNIVERSITY PRESS
Cambridge, New York, Melbourne, Madrid, Cape Town,
Singapore, São Paulo, Delhi, Mexico City

Cambridge University Press
32 Avenue of the Americas, New York, NY 10013-2473, USA

www.cambridge.org
Information on this title: www.cambridge.org/9781107648678

First published 1991
Second edition 1997
Third edition 2005
2nd printing 2012

Printed in Hong Kong, by Golden Cup Printing Company Limited

A catalog record for this publication is available from the British Library.

ISBN 978-1-107-64867-8 Student's Book 1 with Self-study DVD-ROM
ISBN 978-1-107-69443-9 Student's Book 1A with Self-study DVD-ROM
ISBN 978-1-107-67396-0 Student's Book 1B with Self-study DVD-ROM
ISBN 978-1-107-64872-2 Workbook 1
ISBN 978-1-107-61687-5 Workbook 1A
ISBN 978-1-107-69959-5 Workbook 1B
ISBN 978-1-107-69917-5 Teacher's Edition 1 with Assessment Audio CD/CD-ROM
ISBN 978-1-107-64725-1 Class Audio 1 CDs
ISBN 978-1-107-67993-1 Full Contact 1 with Self-study DVD-ROM
ISBN 978-1-107-61136-8 Full Contact 1A with Self-study DVD-ROM
ISBN 978-1-107-63780-1 Full Contact 1B with Self-study DVD-ROM

For a full list of components, visit www. cambridge.org/interchange

Art direction, book design, layout services, and photo research: Integra
Audio production: CityVox, NYC
Video production: Nesson Media Boston, Inc.

Welcome to *Interchange Fourth Edition*, the world's most successful English series!

Interchange offers a complete set of tools for learning how to communicate in English.

Student's Book
with NEW Self-study DVD-ROM

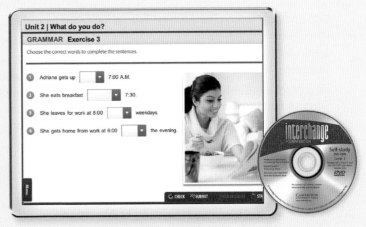

- **Complete video program** with additional **video exercises**

- Additional **vocabulary, grammar, speaking, listening,** and **reading** practice
- Printable **score reports** to submit to teachers

Available online

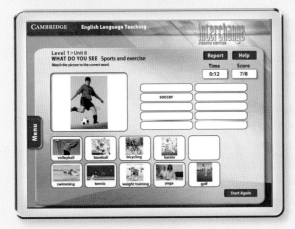

Interchange Arcade

- **Free** self-study website
- **Fun**, interactive, self-scoring activities
- Practice **vocabulary, grammar, listening,** and **reading**
- **MP3s** of the class audio program

Online Workbook

- A variety of **interactive activities** that correspond to each Student's Book lesson
- **Instant feedback** for hundreds of activities
- **Easy to use** with clear, easy-to-follow instructions
- Extra **listening practice**
- Simple tools for teachers to **monitor progress** such as scores, attendance, and time spent online

Authors' acknowledgments

A great number of people contributed to the development of *Interchange Fourth Edition*. Particular thanks are owed to the reviewers using *Interchange, Third Edition* in the following schools and institutes – their insights and suggestions have helped define the content and format of the fourth edition:

Ian Geoffrey Hanley, **The Address Education Center**, Izmir, Turkey

James McBride, **AUA Language Center**, Bangkok, Thailand

Jane Merivale, **Centennial College**, Toronto, Ontario, Canada

Elva Elena Peña Andrade, **Centro de Auto Aprendizaje de Idiomas**, Nuevo León, Mexico

José Paredes, **Centro de Educación Continua de la Escuela Politécnica Nacional** (CEC-EPN), Quito, Ecuador

Chia-jung Tsai, **Changhua University of Education**, Changhua City, Taiwan

Kevin Liang, **Chinese Culture University**, Taipei, Taiwan

Roger Alberto Neira Perez, **Colegio Santo Tomás de Aquino**, Bogotá, Colombia

Teachers at **Escuela Miguel F. Martínez**, Monterrey, Mexico

Maria Virgínia Goulart Borges de Lebron, **Great Idiomas**, São Paulo, Brazil

Gina Kim, **Hoseo University**, Chungnam, South Korea

Heeyong Kim, Seoul, South Korea

Elisa Borges, **IBEU-Rio**, Rio de Janeiro, Brazil

Jason M. Ham, **Inha University**, Incheon, South Korea

Rita de Cássia S. Silva Miranda, **Instituto Batista de Idiomas**, Belo Horizonte, Brazil

Teachers at **Instituto Politécnico Nacional**, Mexico City, Mexico

Victoria M. Roberts and Regina Marie Williams, **Interactive College of Technology**, Chamblee, Georgia, USA

Teachers at **Internacional de Idiomas**, Mexico City, Mexico

Marcelo Serafim Godinho, **Life Idiomas**, São Paulo, Brazil

J. Kevin Varden, **Meiji Gakuin University**, Yokohama, Japan

Rosa Maria Valencia Rodrìguez, Mexico City, Mexico

Chung-Ju Fan, **National Kinmen Institute of Technology**, Kinmen, Taiwan

Shawn Beasom, **Nihon Daigaku**, Tokyo, Japan

Gregory Hadley, **Niigata University of International and Information Studies**, Niigata, Japan

Chris Ruddenklau, **Osaka University of Economics and Law**, Osaka, Japan

Byron Roberts, **Our Lady of Providence Girls' High School**, Xindian City, Taiwan

Simon Banha, **Phil Young's English School**, Curitiba, Brazil

Flávia Gonçalves Carneiro Braathen, **Real English Center**, Viçosa, Brazil

Márcia Cristina Barboza de Miranda, **SENAC**, Recife, Brazil

Raymond Stone, **Seneca College of Applied Arts and Technology**, Toronto, Ontario, Canada

Gen Murai, **Takushoku University**, Tokyo, Japan

Teachers at **Tecnológico de Estudios Superiores de Ecatepec**, Mexico City, Mexico

Teachers at **Universidad Autónoma Metropolitana–Azcapotzalco**, Mexico City, Mexico

Teachers at **Universidad Autónoma de Nuevo León**, Monterrey, Mexico

Mary Grace Killian Reyes, **Universidad Autónoma de Tamaulipas**, Tampico Tamaulipas, Mexico

Teachers at **Universidad Estatal del Valle de Ecatepec**, Mexico City, Mexico

Teachers at **Universidad Nacional Autónoma de Mexico – Zaragoza**, Mexico City, Mexico

Teachers at **Universidad Nacional Autónoma de Mexico – Iztacala**, Mexico City, Mexico

Luz Edith Herrera Diaz, Veracruz, Mexico

Seri Park, **YBM PLS**, Seoul, South Korea

Self-assessment charts revised by Alex Tilbury

Grammar plus written by Karen Davy

Plan of Book 1

Titles/Topics	Speaking	Grammar
UNIT 1 — PAGES 2–7		
Please call me Beth. Introductions and greetings; names, countries, and nationalities	Introducing yourself; introducing someone; checking information; exchanging personal information; saying hello and good-bye	Wh-questions and statements with *be*; questions with *what, where, who,* and *how*; yes/no questions and short answers with *be*; subject pronouns; possessive adjectives
UNIT 2 — PAGES 8–13		
What do you do? Jobs, workplaces, and school; daily schedules; clock time	Describing work and school; asking for and giving opinions; describing daily schedules	Simple present Wh-questions and statements; question: *when*; time expressions: *at, in, on, around, early, late, until, before,* and *after*
PROGRESS CHECK — PAGES 14–15		
UNIT 3 — PAGES 16–21		
How much is it? Shopping and prices; clothing and personal items; colors and materials	Talking about prices; giving opinions; discussing preferences; making comparisons; buying and selling things	Demonstratives: *this, that, these, those; one* and *ones*; questions: *how much* and *which*; comparisons with adjectives
UNIT 4 — PAGES 22–27		
I really like hip-hop. Music, movies, and TV programs; entertainers; invitations and excuses; dates and times	Talking about likes and dislikes; giving opinions; making invitations and excuses	Yes/no and Wh-questions with *do*; question: *what kind*; object pronouns; modal verb *would*; verb + *to* + verb
PROGRESS CHECK — PAGES 28–29		
UNIT 5 — PAGES 30–35		
I come from a big family. Families; typical families	Talking about families and family members; exchanging information about the present; describing family life	Present continuous yes/no and Wh-questions, statements, and short answers; quantifiers: *all,* nearly *all, most, many, a lot of, some, not many,* and *few*; pronoun: *no one*
UNIT 6 — PAGES 36–41		
How often do you exercise? Sports, fitness activities, and exercise; routines	Asking about and describing routines and exercise; talking about frequency; discussing sports and athletes; talking about abilities	Adverbs of frequency: *always, almost always, usually, often, sometimes, hardly ever, almost never,* and *never*; questions: *how often, how long, how well,* and *how good*; short answers
PROGRESS CHECK — PAGES 42–43		
UNIT 7 — PAGES 44–49		
We had a great time! Free-time and weekend activities	Talking about past events; giving opinions about past experiences; talking about vacations	Simple past yes/no and Wh-questions, statements, and short answers with regular and irregular verbs; past of *be*
UNIT 8 — PAGES 50–55		
What's your neighborhood like? Stores and places in a city; neighborhoods; houses and apartments	Asking about and describing locations of places; asking about and describing neighborhoods; asking about quantities	*There is/there are; one, any,* and *some*; prepositions of place; quantifiers; questions: *how many* and *how much*; count and noncount nouns
PROGRESS CHECK — PAGES 56–57		

1 Please call me Beth.

1 CONVERSATION *Where are you from?*

▶ Listen and practice.

David: Hello, I'm David Garza. I'm a new club member.

Beth: Hi. My name is Elizabeth Silva, but please call me Beth.

David: OK. Where are you from, Beth?

Beth: Brazil. How about you?

David: I'm from Mexico.

Beth: Oh, I love Mexico! It's really beautiful.

Beth: Oh, good. Sun-hee is here.

David: Who's Sun-hee?

Beth: She's my classmate. We're in the same math class.

David: Where's she from?

Beth: South Korea. Let's go and say hello. Sorry, what's your last name again? Garcia?

David: Actually, it's Garza.

Beth: How do you spell that?

David: G-A-R-Z-A.

2 SPEAKING *Checking information*

A ▶ Match the questions with the responses. Listen and check. Then practice with a partner. Give your own information.

1. I'm sorry. What's your name again? ....
2. What do people call you? ....
3. How do you spell your last name? ....

a. S-I-L-V-A.
b. It's Elizabeth Silva.
c. Everyone calls me Beth.

B GROUP WORK Introduce yourself with your full name. Use the expressions in part A. Make a list of names for your group.

A: Hi! I'm Yuriko Noguchi.
B: I'm sorry. What's your last name again? . . .

3 CONVERSATION *What's Seoul like?*

A Listen and practice.

Beth: Sun-hee, this is David Garza. He's a new club member from Mexico.

Sun-hee: Nice to meet you, David. I'm Sun-hee Park.

David: Hi. So, you're from South Korea?

Sun-hee: That's right. I'm from Seoul.

David: That's cool. What's Seoul like?

Sun-hee: It's really nice. It's a very exciting city.

B Listen to the rest of the conversation. What city is David from? What's it like?

4 PRONUNCIATION *Linked sounds*

 Listen and practice. Notice how final consonant sounds are often linked to the vowels that follow them.

I'm a new club member.   Sun-hee is over there.   My name is Elizabeth Silva.

5 GRAMMAR FOCUS

Statements with be; possessive adjectives

Statements with **be**	Contractions of **be**	Possessive adjectives
I**'m** from Mexico.	I**'m** = I am	my
You**'re** from Brazil.	you**'re** = you are	your
He**'s** from Japan.	he**'s** = he is	his
She**'s** a new club member.	she**'s** = she is	her
It**'s** an exciting city.	it**'s** = it is	its
We**'re** in the same class.	we**'re** = we are	our
They**'re** my classmates.	they**'re** = they are	their

A Complete these sentences. Then tell a partner about yourself.

1. ...My... name is Mariko Kimura. .... from Japan. .... family is in Osaka. .... brother is a university student. .... name is Kenji.

2. .... name is Antonio. .... from Buenos Aires. .... a really nice city. .... sister is a student here, too. .... parents are in Argentina right now.

3. .... Katherine, but everyone calls me Katie. .... last name is Martin. .... a student at City College. .... parents are on vacation this week. .... in Los Angeles.

B Complete these questions. Then practice with a partner.

1. A: ....Who's....... that?
    B: Oh, that's Miss West.

2. A: .... she from?
    B: She's from Miami.

3. A: .... her first name?
    B: It's Celia.

4. A: .... the two students over there?
    B: Their names are Jeremy and Karen.

5. A: .... they from?
    B: They're from Vancouver, Canada.

6. A: .... they .... ?
    B: They're shy, but very friendly.

C **GROUP WORK** Write five questions about your classmates. Then ask and answer the questions.

What's your last name?
Where's Ming from?

6 SNAPSHOT

Sources: www.familyeducation.com; www.time.com

Which greetings are typical in your country?
Can you write the name of a country for each greeting?
What are other ways to greet people?

7 CONVERSATION *How's it going?*

▶ Listen and practice.

Sun-hee: Hey, David. How's it going?
David: Fine, thanks. How are you?
Sun-hee: Pretty good. So, are your classes interesting this semester?
David: Yes, they are. I really love chemistry.
Sun-hee: Chemistry? Are you and Beth in the same class?
David: No, we aren't. My class is in the morning. Her class is in the afternoon.
Sun-hee: Listen, I'm on my way to the cafeteria now. Are you free?
David: Sure. Let's go.

8 GRAMMAR FOCUS

Yes/No questions and short answers with be ▶

Are you free?	Yes, I **am**.	No, I**'m not**.
Is David from Mexico?	Yes, he **is**.	No, he**'s not**./No, he **isn't**.
Is Beth's class in the morning?	Yes, it **is**.	No, it**'s not**./No, it **isn't**.
Are you and Beth in the same class?	Yes, we **are**.	No, we**'re not**./No, we **aren't**.
Are your classes interesting?	Yes, they **are**.	No, they**'re not**./No, they **aren't**.

A Complete these conversations. Then practice with a partner.

1. A: ......*Is*...... Ms. Gray from the United States?
   B: Yes, she .... from Chicago.

2. A: .... English class at 10:00?
   B: No, it .... at 11:00.

3. A: .... you and Monique from France?
   B: Yes, we .... from Paris.

4. A: .... Mr. and Mrs. Tavares American?
   B: No, they .... Brazilian.

B Answer these questions. If you answer "no," give the correct information. Then ask your partner the questions.

1. Are you from the United States? ....
2. Is your teacher from Canada? ....
3. Is your English class in the morning? ....
4. Are you and your best friend the same age? ....

C GROUP WORK Write five questions about your classmates. Then ask and answer the questions.

> Are Cindy and Brian from Los Angeles?

9 WORD POWER Hello and good-bye

A Do you know these expressions? Which ones are "hellos" and which ones are "good-byes"? Complete the chart. Add expressions of your own.

✓ Bye.
✓ Good morning.
  Good night.
  Have a good day.
  Hey.
  Hi.

How are you?
How's it going?
See you later.
See you tomorrow.
Talk to you later.
What's up?

Hello	Good-bye
Good morning.	Bye.

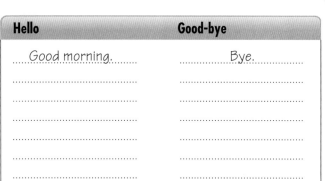

B Match each expression with the best response.

1. Have a good day.
2. Hi. How are you?
3. What's up?
4. Good morning.

a. Oh, not much.
b. Thank you. You, too.
c. Good morning.
d. Pretty good, thanks.

C CLASS ACTIVITY Practice saying hello. Then practice saying good-bye.

A: Hi, Aki. How's it going?
B: Pretty good, thanks. How are you?

10 LISTENING What's your last name again?

Listen to the conversations. Complete the information about each person.

	First name	Last name	Where from?
1.	Chris		
2.		Sanchez	
3.	Min-ho		

11 INTERCHANGE 1 Getting to know you

Find out about your classmates. Go to Interchange 1 on page 114.

What's in a Name?

Look at the names in the article. Do you know any people with these names? What are they like?

Your name is very important. When you think of yourself, you probably think of your name first. It is an important part of your identity.

Right now, the two most popular names for babies in the United States are "Jacob" for boys and "Emma" for girls. Why are these names popular? And why are other names unpopular?

Names can become popular because of famous actors, TV or book characters, or athletes. Popular names suggest very positive things. Unpopular names suggest negative things. Surprisingly, people generally agree on the way they feel about names. Here are some common opinions about names from a recent survey.

HELLO
my name is
_____

Boys' names

George: average, boring
Jacob: creative, friendly
Michael: good-looking, athletic
Stanley: nerdy, serious

Girls' names

Betty: old-fashioned, average
Emma: independent, adventurous
Jane: plain, ordinary
Nicole: beautiful, intelligent

So why do parents give their children unpopular names? One reason is tradition. Many people are named after a family member. Of course, opinions can change over time. A name that is unpopular now may become popular in the future. That's good news for all the Georges and Bettys out there!

A Read the article. Then check (✓) the statements that are true.

1. Your name is part of your identity.
2. People often feel the same way about a particular name.
3. Boys' names are more popular than girls' names.
4. People are often named after family members.
5. Opinions about names can change.

B According to the article, which names suggest positive things? Which suggest negative things? Complete the chart.

Positive names		Negative names	
....	....	....	....
....	....	....	....

C PAIR WORK What names are popular in your country? Why are they popular?

2 What do you do?

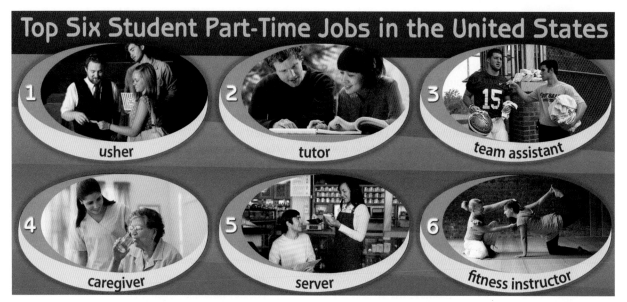

Top Six Student Part-Time Jobs in the United States

1 usher
2 tutor
3 team assistant
4 caregiver
5 server
6 fitness instructor

Source: www.snagajob.com

Which jobs are easy? Which are difficult? Why?
What's your opinion? Are these good jobs for students?
What are some other student jobs?

2 WORD POWER

A Complete the word map with jobs from the list.

✓ accountant
✓ cashier
  chef
✓ dancer
✓ flight attendant
  musician
  pilot
  receptionist
  server
  singer
  tour guide
  website designer

Office work
accountant

Food service
cashier

Jobs

Travel industry
flight attendant

Entertainment business
dancer

B Add two more jobs to each category. Then compare with a partner.

8

3 SPEAKING Work and workplaces

A Look at the pictures. Match the information in columns A, B, and C.

A	B	C
a salesperson	builds houses	in a restaurant
a chef	cares for patients	for a construction company
a mechanic	writes stories	in a hospital
a carpenter	cooks food	in a garage
a reporter	fixes cars	**in a department store**
a nurse	**sells clothes**	for a newspaper

B **PAIR WORK** Take turns describing each person's job.

A: She's a salesperson. She sells clothes. She works in a department store.

B: And he's a chef. He . . .

4 CONVERSATION Where do you work?

A ▶ Listen and practice.

Jason: Where do you work, Andrea?

Andrea: I work at Thomas Cook Travel.

Jason: Oh, really? What do you do there?

Andrea: I'm a guide. I take people on tours to countries in South America, like Peru.

Jason: How interesting!

Andrea: Yeah, it's a great job. I really love it. And what do you do?

Jason: Oh, I'm a student. I have a part-time job, too.

Andrea: Where do you work?

Jason: In a fast-food restaurant.

Andrea: Which restaurant?

Jason: Hamburger Heaven.

B ▶ Listen to the rest of the conversation. What does Jason do, exactly? How does he like his job?

5 GRAMMAR FOCUS

Simple present Wh-questions and statements ▶

			I/You	**He/She**
What do you **do**?	I**'m** a student. I **have** a part-time job, too.		work	works
Where do you **work**?	I **work** at Hamburger Heaven.		take	takes
Where do you **go** to school?	I **go** to the University of Texas.		study	studies
			teach	teaches
What does Andrea **do**?	She's a guide. She **takes** people on tours.		do	does
Where does she **work**?	She **works** at Thomas Cook Travel.		go	goes
How does she **like** it?	She **loves** it.		have	has

A Complete these conversations. Then practice with a partner.

1. A: What ....*do*.... you ....*do*.... ?
   B: I'm a full-time student. I study the violin.
   A: And .... do you .... to school?
   B: I .... to the New York School of Music.
   A: Wow! .... do you like your classes?
   B: I .... them a lot.

2. A: What .... Tanya do?
   B: She's a teacher. She .... an art class
      at a school in Denver.
   A: And what about Ryan? Where .... he work?
   B: He .... for a big computer company in
      San Francisco.
   A: .... does he do, exactly?
   B: He's a website designer. He .... fantastic
      websites.

B **PAIR WORK** What do you know about these jobs?
Complete the chart. Then write sentences about each job.

A reporter	A flight attendant	A teacher
works for a newspaper	....	....
interviews people	....	....
writes stories	....	....

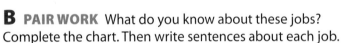
A reporter works for a newspaper, interviews people, and writes stories.

C **PAIR WORK** Ask your partner questions like these about work
and school. Take notes to use in Exercise 6.

What do you do?	Do you go to school?	How do you like . . . ?
Where do you live?	Do you have a job?	What's your favorite . . . ?

6 *WRITING* A biography

A Use your notes from Exercise 5 to write a biography of your partner. Don't use your partner's name. Use *he* or *she* instead.

> My partner is a student. She lives near the university. She studies fashion design at the Fashion Institute. Her favorite class is History of Design. She has a part-time job in a clothing store. She loves her job and . . .

B CLASS ACTIVITY Pass your biographies around the class. Guess who each biography is about.

7 *CONVERSATION* I start work at five.

A Listen and practice.

Kevin: So, do you usually come to the gym in the morning?

Allie: Yeah, I do. I usually come here at 10:00.

Kevin: Really? What time do you go to work?

Allie: Oh, I work in the afternoon. I start work at five.

Kevin: Wow, that's late. When do you get home at night?

Allie: I usually get home at midnight.

Kevin: Midnight? That *is* late. What do you do, exactly?

Allie: I'm a chef. I work at the Pink Elephant.

Kevin: That's my favorite restaurant! By the way, I'm Kevin. . . .

B Listen to the rest of the conversation. What time does Kevin get up? start work?

8 *PRONUNCIATION* Syllable stress

A Listen and practice. Notice which syllable has the main stress.

● ○	● ○ ○	○ ● ○
dancer	salesperson	accountant
....	....	....
....	....	....

B Which stress pattern do these words have? Add them to the columns in part A. Then listen and check.

carpenter   caregiver   musician   reporter   server   tutor

9 GRAMMAR FOCUS

				Expressing clock time
I get up	**at** 6:00	**in** the morning	**on** weekdays.	6:00
I go to bed	**around** ten	**in** the evening	**on** weeknights.	six
I leave work	**early**	**in** the afternoon	**on** weekends.	six o'clock
I get home	**late**	**at** night	**on** Fridays.	6:00 A.M. = 6:00 in the morning
I stay up	**until** midnight	**on** Saturdays.		6:00 P.M. = 6:00 in the evening
I exercise	**before** noon	**on** Saturdays.		
I wake up	**after** noon	**on** Sundays.		

A Circle the correct words.

1. I get up **at** / **until** six **at** / **on** weekdays.
2. I have lunch **at** / **early** 11:30 **in** / **on** Mondays.
3. I have a little snack **in** / **around** 10:00 **in** / **at** night.
4. **In** / **On** Fridays, I leave school **early** / **before**.
5. I stay up **before** / **until** 1:00 A.M. **in** / **on** weekends.
6. I sleep **until** / **around** noon **in** / **on** Sundays.

B Rewrite the sentences in part A so that they are true for you. Then compare with a partner.

C PAIR WORK Take turns asking and answering these questions.

1. Which days do you get up early? late?
2. What's something you do before 8:00 in the morning?
3. What's something you do on Saturday evenings?
4. What do you do only on Sundays?

10 LISTENING Daily schedules

A ▶ Listen to Greg, Megan, and Lori talk about their daily schedules. Complete the chart.

	Job	Gets up at . . .	Gets home at . . .	Goes to bed at . . .
Greg	mechanic			
Megan		7:00 a.m.		
Lori				

B CLASS ACTIVITY Who do you think has the best daily schedule? Why?

11 INTERCHANGE 2 Common ground

Find out about your classmates' schedules. Go to Interchange 2 on page 115.

Why do you need a job?

Scan the profiles. Who is in high school? Who is in college? Who is a new parent?

These people need jobs. Read about their schedules, experience, and why they need a job.

Eddie Chen

I'm 16 now, and my parents don't give me an allowance anymore. I want to earn some money because I like to go out with my friends on the weekend. I go to school at 8:00 and get home around 4:30. My parents own a restaurant, so I know a little about restaurant work.

Julia Brown

I study French and want to be a teacher someday. I have classes all day on Monday, Tuesday, and Thursday, and on Wednesday and Friday afternoons. I usually study on weekends. I need a job because college is really expensive! I don't have any experience, but I'm a fast learner.

Denise Parker

My husband is an accountant and makes good money, but we don't save very much. We live in a small apartment, and we have a new baby. We want to save money to buy a house. I take care of the baby, so I need a job I can do at home. I can type well, and I have a new computer.

A Read the article. Why do these people need jobs? Check (✓) the correct boxes.

	Julia	Denise	Eddie
1. To save money	☐	☐	☐
2. To pay for college	☐	☐	☐
3. To go out on the weekend	☐	☐	☐
4. To buy a house	☐	☐	☐

B PAIR WORK Choose the best job for each person. Explain why.

Chef	**English Tutor**	**Caregiver**
French and Italian cooking *Weekends only*	*Flexible work hours* *$10 an hour*	*Work with children* *Earn great money*
Server	**Receptionist**	**Online Salesperson**
Evenings only *Experience a plus*	*Mornings and afternoons* *No experience necessary*	*Work at home* *Earn up to $20 an hour*

Units 1–2 Progress check

SELF-ASSESSMENT

How well can you do these things? Check (✓) the boxes.

I can	Very well	OK	A little
Make an introduction and use basic greeting expressions (Ex. 1)	☐	☐	☐
Show I didn't understand and ask for repetition (Ex. 1)	☐	☐	☐
Ask and answer questions about myself and other people (Ex. 2)	☐	☐	☐
Ask and answer questions about work (Ex. 3, 4)	☐	☐	☐
Ask and answer questions about habits and routines (Ex. 5)	☐	☐	☐

 ROLE PLAY *Introductions*

A **PAIR WORK** You are talking to someone at school. Have a conversation.

A: Hi. How are you?
B: . . .
A: By the way, my name is . . .
B: I'm sorry. What's your name again?
A: . . .
B: I'm . . . . Are you a student here?
A: . . . And how about you?
B: . . .
A: Oh, really? And where are you from?

B **GROUP WORK** Join another pair.
Introduce your partner.

 SPEAKING *Interview*

Write questions for these answers. Then use the questions to interview a classmate.

1.	What's	?	My name is Keiko Kawakami.
2.		?	I'm from Osaka, Japan.
3.		?	Yes, my classes are very interesting.
4.		?	My favorite class is English.
5.		?	No, my teacher isn't American.
6.		?	My classmates are very nice.
7.		?	My best friend is Maria.

3 SPEAKING *What a job!*

A What do you know about these jobs? List three things each person does.

receptionist

tour guide

cashier

teacher

takes messages

....

....

....

B GROUP WORK Compare your lists. Take turns asking about the jobs.

4 LISTENING *Work and school*

A Listen to James and Lindsey talk at a party. Complete the chart.

	James	Lindsey
What do you do?	....	....
Where do you work/study?	....	....
How do you like your job/classes?	....	....
What do you do after work/school?	....	....

B PAIR WORK Practice the questions in part A. Answer with your own information.

5 SURVEY *My perfect day*

A Imagine your perfect day. Complete the chart with your own answers.

What time do you get up?	....
What do you do after you get up?	....
Where do you go?	....
What do you do in the evening?	....
When do you go to bed?	....

B PAIR WORK Talk about your perfect day. Answer any questions.

WHAT'S NEXT?

Look at your Self-assessment again. Do you need to review anything?

3 How much is it?

1 SNAPSHOT

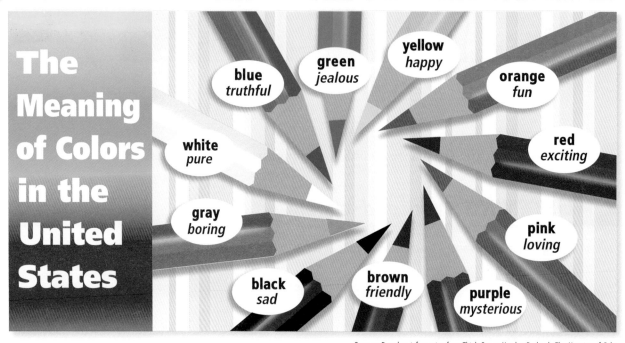

The Meaning of Colors in the United States

blue
truthful

green
jealous

yellow
happy

orange
fun

white
pure

red
exciting

gray
boring

pink
loving

black
sad

brown
friendly

purple
mysterious

Sources: Based on information from Think Quest; Hewlett-Packard, *The Meaning of Color*

Which words have a positive meaning? Which have a negative meaning?
What meanings do these colors have for you?
What does your favorite color make you think of?

2 CONVERSATION *It's really pretty.*

A ▶ Listen and practice.

Salesclerk: Can I help you?
Customer: Yes, thank you. How much are these gloves?
Salesclerk: The gray ones? They're $18.
Customer: Oh, that's not bad. Do they come in black?
Salesclerk: No, sorry, just gray.
Customer: OK. Um, how much is that scarf?
Salesclerk: Which one? The blue and orange one?
Customer: No, the yellow one.
Salesclerk: Let's see . . . it's $24.95.
Customer: It's really pretty. I'll take it.

B ▶ Listen to the rest of the conversation. What else does the customer look at? Does she buy it?

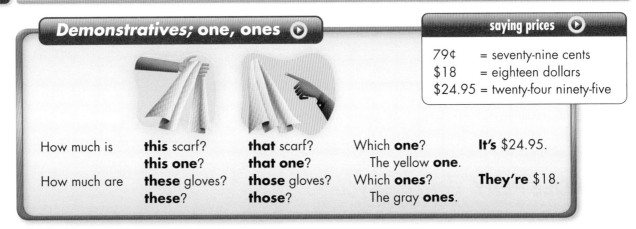

Demonstratives; one, ones ▶

saying prices ▶

79¢	= seventy-nine cents
$18	= eighteen dollars
$24.95	= twenty-four ninety-five

How much is	**this** scarf?	**that** scarf?	Which **one**?	**It's** $24.95.
	this one?	**that one**?	The yellow **one**.	
How much are	**these** gloves?	**those** gloves?	Which **ones**?	**They're** $18.
	these?	**those**?	The gray **ones**.	

A Complete these conversations. Then practice with a partner.

1

A: Excuse me. How much
   are ....*those*.... jeans?
B: Which .... ? Do you
   mean .... ?
A: No, the light blue ....
B: Oh, ... are $59.95.
A: Wow! That's expensive!

2

A: How much is .... backpack?
B: Which .... ?
A: The red ....
B: It's $36.99. But ....
   green .... is only $22.25.
A: That's not bad. Can I see it, please?

B **PAIR WORK** Add prices to the items. Then ask and answer questions.

A: How much are these sunglasses?
B: Which ones?
A: The pink ones.
B: They're $86.99.
A: That's expensive!

useful expressions

That's cheap.
That's reasonable.
That's OK/not bad.
That's expensive.

4 PRONUNCIATION *Sentence stress*

A ▶ Listen and practice. Notice that the important words in a sentence have more stress.

Excuse me.   That's expensive.   I'll take it.   Do you mean these?

B **PAIR WORK** Practice the conversations in Exercise 3, part B again. Pay attention to the sentence stress.

5 ROLE PLAY *Can I help you?*

A **PAIR WORK** Put items "for sale" on your desk, such as notebooks, watches, phones, or bags.

Student A: You are a salesclerk. Answer the customer's questions.
Student B: You are a customer. Ask the price of each item. Say if you want to buy it.

    A: Can I help you?
    B: Yes. I like these sunglasses. How much are they?
    A: Which ones?

B Change roles and try the role play again.

6 LISTENING *Look at this!*

A ▶ Listen to two friends shopping. Write the color and price for each item.

Item	Color	Price	Do they buy it?	
			Yes	No
1. phone	....	....	☐	☐
2. watch	....	....	☐	☐
3. sunglasses	....	....	☐	☐
4. T-shirt	....	....	☐	☐

B ▶ Listen again. Do they buy the items? Check (✓) Yes or No.

7 INTERCHANGE 3 *Flea market*

See what kinds of deals you can make as a buyer and a seller.
Go to Interchange 3 on pages 116–117.

8 WORD POWER *Materials*

A What are these things made of? Label each one. Use the words from the list.

cotton   gold   leather   plastic
rubber   silk   silver   wool

1. a ....*silk*.... tie   2. a .... bracelet   3. a .... ring   4. a .... shirt

5. a .... jacket   6. .... earrings   7. .... boots   8. .... socks

B PAIR WORK What other materials are the things in part A sometimes made of? Make a list.

C CLASS ACTIVITY Which materials can you find in your classroom?

"Pedro has a cotton shirt, and Ellen has leather shoes."

9 CONVERSATION *I prefer the blue one.*

A ⊙ Listen and practice.

Brett: These wool sweaters are really nice.
       Which one do you like better?
 Lisa: Let's see . . . I like the green one more.
Brett: The green one? Why?
 Lisa: It looks warmer.
Brett: That's true, but I think I prefer the blue one.
       It's more stylish than the green one.
 Lisa: Hmm. There's no price tag.
Brett: Excuse me. How much is this sweater?
Clerk: It's $139. Would you like to try it on?
Brett: Uh, no. That's OK. But thanks anyway.
Clerk: You're welcome.

B ⊙ Listen to the rest of the conversation.
What does Brett buy? What does Lisa think of it?

Preferences; comparisons with adjectives ⊙

Which sweater do you **prefer**?
  I **prefer** the blue one.   It's **nicer than** the green one.
Which one do you **like more**?
  I **like** the blue one **more**. It's **prettier than** the green one.
Which one do you **like better**?
  I **like** the blue one **better**. It's **more stylish than** the green one.

Spelling
cheap ⟶ cheaper
nice ⟶ nicer
pretty ⟶ prettier
big ⟶ bigger

A Complete these conversations. Then practice with a partner.

1. A: Which of these jackets do you like more?
   B: I prefer the leather one. The design is .... (nice), and it looks .... (expensive) the wool one.

2. A: These T-shirts are nice. Which one do you prefer?
   B: I like the green and white one better. The colors are .... (pretty). It's .... (attractive) the gray and black one.

3. A: Which earrings do you like better?
   B: I like the silver ones more. They're .... (big) the gold ones. And they're .... (cheap).

B **PAIR WORK** Compare the things in part A. Give your own opinions.

A: Which jacket do you like more?
B: I like the wool one better. The color is prettier.

useful expressions

The color is prettier.
The design is nicer.
The style is more attractive.
The material is better.

 WRITING *Comparing prices*

How much do these things cost in your country? Complete the chart.
Then compare the prices in your country with the prices in the U.S.

	Price in my country	Price in the U.S.
a cup of coffee	....	$1.40
a movie ticket	....	$12.50
a paperback novel	....	$8.95
a video game	....	$50.00

Many things are more expensive in my country than in the United States. For example, a cup of coffee costs about $2.00 at home. In the U.S., it's cheaper. It's only $1.40. A movie ticket costs . . .

Tools for Better Shopping

Scan the article. Find the names of popular websites. Do you use any of them for shopping?

1 Do you like to shop online? Like millions of people, you want to find the best things for the best price. There are so many choices that it can be difficult to find the things you need and want. Here's where technology comes in! Popular websites like Facebook and Twitter aren't just for social networking anymore.

2 The websites Facebook and Twitter are popular because people can connect to friends and get their most recent news. But people also use these sites as powerful shopping tools. Members can ask about an item and then get opinions from people they trust. Twitterers can also search for news from other users and then find stores nearby that sell the item.

3 Another helpful shopping tool is the smartphone. Smartphone users can go into a store, find an item they like, and then type the item number into their smartphone. They can compare prices, read reviews, and make better decisions about their purchase. Many people find a better price online or at another store. People often want to see and touch an item before they buy. They can do just that – and pay a lower price, too.

4 But you don't have to be a Facebook or Twitter member or have a smartphone to find a bargain. Websites like Shopzilla compare prices, give reviews, and find stores near you with the best bargains. Google does all these things but also lets you buy items directly through its site. Be a smart shopper. The information you need is at your fingertips!

A Read the article. Answer these questions. Then write the number of the paragraph where you find each answer.

.... a. How are Shopzilla and Google similar? ....
.... b. What are Twitter users called? ....
.... c. How do smartphones help find bargains? ....
.... d. What are two social networking sites? ....

B According to the article, which shopping tools do these things?
Check (✓) the correct boxes.

	Facebook	Twitter	Smartphone	Shopzilla	Google
1. get opinions from friends	☐	☐	☐	☐	☐
2. find product reviews	☐	☐	☐	☐	☐
3. compare prices	☐	☐	☐	☐	☐
4. find stores with items you want	☐	☐	☐	☐	☐
5. buy items directly	☐	☐	☐	☐	☐

C **PAIR WORK** Do you shop mostly in stores or online? How do you find good prices?

4 I really like hip-hop.

1 SNAPSHOT

Music Sales in the United States

Rock 32%
Other 15%
Classical 2%
Jazz 1%
Gospel 7%
Hip-hop 11%
R&B 10%
Pop 9%
Country 12%
New Age 1%

Source: The Recording Industry Association of America, *2008 Consumer Profile*

Listen and number the musical styles from 1 to 9.
Which of these styles of music are popular in your country?
What other kinds of music are popular in your country?

2 WORD POWER

A Complete the word map with words from the list.

action   reality show
electronic   reggae
game show   salsa
heavy metal   science fiction
horror   soap opera
musical   talk show

B Add two more words to each category.
Then compare with a partner.

C GROUP WORK Number the items
in each list from 1 (you like it the most)
to 6 (you like it the least). Then compare
your ideas.

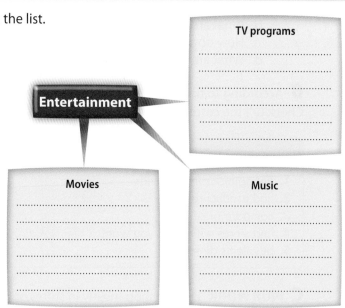

Entertainment

TV programs

Movies

Music

3 CONVERSATION *Who's your favorite singer?*

A ▶ Listen and practice.

Marissa: Do you like country music, Brian?
   Brian: No, I don't like it very much. Do you?
Marissa: Yeah, I do. I'm a big fan of Taylor Swift.
   Brian: I think I know her. Does she play the guitar?
Marissa: Yes, she does. She's a really good musician.
            So, what kind of music do you like?
   Brian: I really like hip-hop.
Marissa: Oh, yeah? Who's your favorite singer?
   Brian: Jay-Z. Do you like him?
Marissa: No, I don't. I don't like hip-hop very much.

B ▶ Listen to the rest of the conversation. Who is Brian's favorite group? Does Marissa like them?

4 GRAMMAR FOCUS

Simple present questions; short answers ▶

		Object pronouns
Do you **like** country music? Yes, I **do**. I love it. No, I **don't**. I don't like it very much.	**What kind of** music **do** you **like**? I really like hip-hop.	me you him
Does she **play** the piano? Yes, she **does**. She plays very well. No, she **doesn't**. She doesn't play an instrument.	**What does** she **play**? She plays the guitar.	her it us
Do they **like** Green Day? Yes, they **do**. They like them a lot. No, they **don't**. They don't like them at all.	**Who do** they **like**? They like Coldplay.	them

Complete these conversations. Then practice with a partner.

1. A: I like Kings of Leon a lot. .... you
       know .... ?
   B: Yes, I .... , and I love this song. Let's
       download ....
2. A: .... you like science fiction movies?
   B: Yes, I .... I like .... very much.
3. A: .... Kevin and Emma like soap operas?
   B: Kevin .... , but Emma .... She
       hates ....
4. A: What kind of music .... Noriko like?
   B: Classical music. She loves Yo-Yo Ma.
   A: Yeah, he's amazing. I like .... a lot.

Kings of Leon

I really like hip-hop. ▪ 23

5 PRONUNCIATION *Intonation in questions*

A ▶ Listen and practice. Yes/No questions usually have rising intonation. Wh-questions usually have falling intonation.

Do you like pop music?

What kind of music do you like?

B PAIR WORK Practice these questions.

Do you like TV?   What programs do you like?
Do you like video games?   What games do you like?
Do you play a musical instrument?   What instrument do you play?

6 SPEAKING *Entertainment survey*

A GROUP WORK Write five questions about entertainment and entertainers.
Then ask and answer your questions in groups.

What kinds of . . . do you like?
   (music, TV programs, video games)
Do you like . . . ?
   (reggae, game shows, action movies)
Who's your favorite . . . ?
   (singer, actor, athlete)

B GROUP WORK Complete this information about your group.
Ask any additional questions.

Our Group Favorites
What's your favorite kind of . . . ?
music ....
movie ....
TV program ....
What's your favorite . . . ?
song ....
movie ....
video game ....
Who's your favorite . . . ?
singer ....
actor ....
athlete ....

Utada Hikaru

reality show

Cristiano Ronaldo

3-D movie

C CLASS ACTIVITY Read your group's list to
the class. Find out the class favorites.

7 LISTENING *Who's my date?*

A  Listen to four people on a TV game show. Three men want to invite Linda on a date. What kinds of things do they like? Complete the chart.

	Music	Movies	TV programs
Bill	....	....	....
John	....	....	....
Tony	....	....	....
Linda	....	....	....

B CLASS ACTIVITY Who do you think is the best date for Linda? Why?

8 CONVERSATION *An invitation*

A ⊙ Listen and practice.

Dave: I have tickets to the soccer match on Friday night. Would you like to go?

Susan: Thanks. I'd love to. What time does it start?

Dave: At 8:00.

Susan: That sounds great. So, do you want to have dinner at 6:00?

Dave: Uh, I'd like to, but I have to work late.

Susan: Oh, that's OK. Let's just meet at the stadium before the match, around 7:30.

Dave: OK. Why don't we meet at the gate?

Susan: That sounds fine. See you there.

B ⊙ Listen to Dave and Susan at the soccer match. Which team does each person like?

I really like hip-hop. ▪ 25

9 GRAMMAR FOCUS

> **Would; verb + to + verb** ▶
>
> | **Would** you **like to go** out on Friday? | **Would** you **like to go** to a soccer match? | *Contraction* |
> |---|---|---|
> | Yes, I **would**. | I**'d like to**, but I **have to work** late. | I**'d** = I would |
> | Yes, I**'d love to**. Thanks. | I**'d like to**, but I **need to save** money. | |
> | | I**'d like to**, but I **want to visit** my parents. | |

A Respond to three invitations. Then write three invitations for the given responses.

1. A: I have tickets to the baseball game on Saturday. Would you like to go?
   B: ....

2. A: Would you like to come over for dinner tomorrow night?
   B: ....

3. A: Would you like to go to a pop concert with me this weekend?
   B: ....

4. A: ....
   ....
   B: Yes, I'd love to. Thank you!

5. A: ....
   ....
   B: Well, I'd like to, but I have to study.

6. A: ....
   ....
   B: Yes, I would. They're my favorite band.

B **PAIR WORK** Ask and answer the questions in part A. Give your own responses.

C **PAIR WORK** Think of three things you would like to do. Then invite a partner to do them with you. Your partner responds and asks follow-up questions like these:

When is it?   What time does it start?   When does it end?   Where is it?

10 WRITING A text message

A What does this text message say?

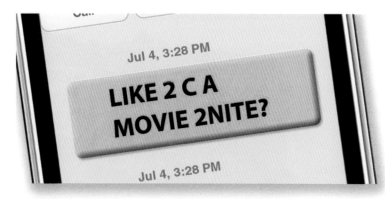

Jul 4, 3:28 PM

LIKE 2 C A MOVIE 2NITE?

Jul 4, 3:28 PM

text message abbreviations			
M	= am	L8	= late
U	= you	W8	= wait
R	= are	GR8	= great
C	= see	THX	= thanks
4	= for	LUV	= love
2	= to	NITE	= night

B **GROUP WORK** Write a text message to each person in your group. Then exchange messages. Write a response to each message.

11 INTERCHANGE 4 Are you free this weekend?

Make weekend plans with your classmates. Go to Interchange 4 on page 118.

Fergie of the Black Eyed Peas

Scan the article and look at the pictures. In what year did each event take place?

She has many hit singles and several Grammy awards with her band the Black Eyed Peas. She has fans all over the world. She's a singer, a rapper, a songwriter, a fashion designer, and an actress. Her name is Stacy Ann Ferguson, but her fans call her Fergie.

Here are some highlights of Fergie's life and career.

▶ **1975** Fergie is born on March 27 in California.
▶ **1984** Fergie starts acting, doing the voice of Sally in the *Peanuts* cartoons. She also stars in the popular TV show *Kids Incorporated*, with actress Jennifer Love Hewitt.
▶ **1991** Fergie forms the all-female band Wild Orchid.
▶ **2003** Fergie records a song with the band Black Eyed Peas. The band likes her, and she records five more songs on the album.
▶ **2004** Fergie joins the Black Eyed Peas.
▶ **2005** Fergie and the Black Eyed Peas win their first Grammy award for "Let's Get It Started."
▶ **2006** Fergie makes a solo album and has six big hits. "Big Girls Don't Cry" is her first worldwide number one single.
▶ **2008** Fergie records "That Ain't Cool" with Japanese R&B singer Kumi Koda. She becomes famous in Japan.
▶ **2009** Fergie acts and sings in the movie *Nine*.
▶ **2010** Fergie and the Black Eyed Peas perform five songs at the 2010 World Cup celebration concert in South Africa.

Fergie says she's the "luckiest girl in the world." Why? Her song "Glamorous" says it all: "All the fans, I'd like to thank. Thank you really though, 'cause I remember yesterday when I dreamed about the days when I'd rock on MTV...."

▲ performing at the World Cup

▲ on the TV show *Kids Incorporated*

▲ on stage with the Black Eyed Peas

A Read the article. Then number these sentences from 1 (first event) to 8 (last event).

.... a. She sings at the World Cup concert.
.... b. She is born in California.
.... c. She acts and sings in a movie.
.... d. Her band wins its first Grammy.
.... e. She forms her first band.
.... f. She is on TV with Jennifer Love Hewitt.
.... g. She becomes very popular in Japan.
.... h. She has her first worldwide number one song.

B PAIR WORK Who is your favorite musician? What do you know about his or her life?

Units 3–4 Progress check

SELF-ASSESSMENT

How well can you do these things? Check (✓) the boxes.

I can	Very well	OK	A little
Give and understand information about prices (Ex. 1)	☐	☐	☐
Say what I like and dislike (Ex. 1, 2, 3)	☐	☐	☐
Explain what I like or dislike about something (Ex. 2)	☐	☐	☐
Describe and compare objects and possessions (Ex. 2)	☐	☐	☐
Make and respond to invitations (Ex. 4)	☐	☐	☐

1 LISTENING *Weekend sale*

A   Listen to a commercial for Dave's Discount Store. Circle the correct prices.

leather pants	wool pants	silk shirt	laptop computer
$19	$15	$14	$1,015
$90	$50	$40	$1,050

DAVE'S DISCOUNT STORE

cotton shirt	desktop computer
$18	$813
$80	$830

B **PAIR WORK** What do you think of the items in part A? Give your own opinions.

2 ROLE PLAY *Shopping trip*

Student A: Choose things from Exercise 1 for your family. Ask for Student B's opinion.

Student B: Help Student A choose presents for his or her family.

> A: I want to buy a computer for my parents. Which one do you like better?
> B: Well, I like the laptop better. It's nicer, and . . .

Change roles and try the role play again.

SURVEY *Likes and dislikes*

A Write answers to these questions.

	Me	My classmate
When do you usually watch TV?		
What kinds of TV programs do you like?		
Do you like game shows?		
Do you listen to the radio?		
Who is your favorite singer?		
What do you think of heavy metal?		
What is your favorite movie?		
Do you like musicals?		
What kinds of movies do you dislike?		

B **CLASS ACTIVITY** Find someone who has the same answers. Go around the class. Write a classmate's name only once!

4 **SPEAKING** *What an excuse!*

A Make up three invitations to interesting activities. Write them on cards.

> *I want to see the frog races*
> *tomorrow. They're at the park*
> *at 2:00. Would you like to go?*

B Write three response cards. One is an acceptance card, and two are refusals. Think of silly or unusual excuses.

> *That sounds great! What*
> *time do you want to meet?*

> *I'd like to, but I have to*
> *wash my cat tomorrow.*

> *I'd love to, but I want*
> *to take my bird to a*
> *singing contest.*

C **GROUP WORK** Shuffle the invitation cards together and the response cards together. Take three cards from each pile. Then invite people to do the things on your invitation cards. Use the response cards to accept or refuse.

WHAT'S NEXT?

Look at your Self-assessment again. Do you need to review anything?

5 I come from a big family.

A Look at Sam's family tree. How are these people related to him?
Add the words to the family tree.

cousin
daughter
father
grandmother
niece
sister-in-law
uncle
wife

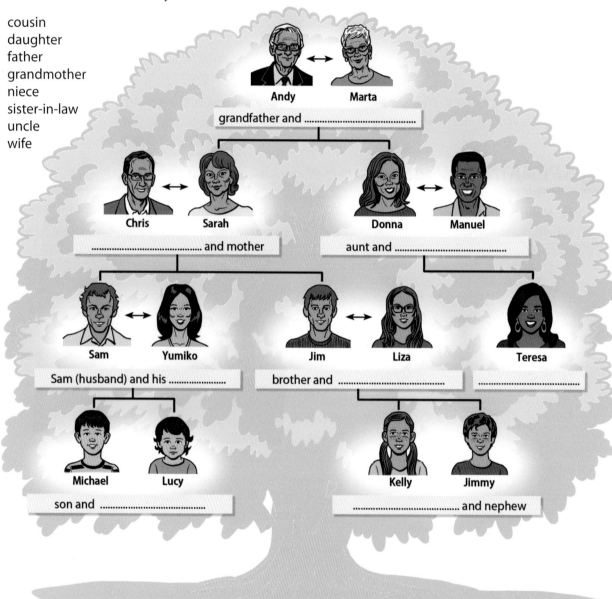

Andy ↔ Marta

grandfather and ....

Chris ↔ Sarah   Donna ↔ Manuel

.... and mother   aunt and ....

Sam ↔ Yumiko   Jim ↔ Liza   Teresa

Sam (husband) and his ....   brother and ....

Michael   Lucy   Kelly   Jimmy

son and .... and nephew

B Draw your family tree (or a friend's family tree). Then take turns talking
about your families. Ask follow-up questions to get more information.

A: There are five people in my family. I have two brothers and a sister.
B: How old is your sister?

2 LISTENING *How are they related?*

▶ Listen to four conversations about famous people. How is the second person related to the first person?

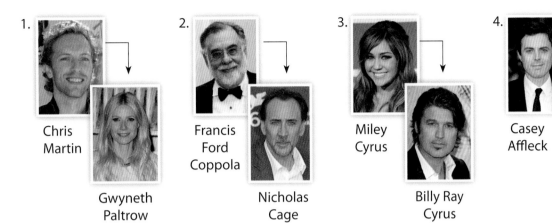

1. Chris Martin → Gwyneth Paltrow

....

2. Francis Ford Coppola → Nicholas Cage

....

3. Miley Cyrus → Billy Ray Cyrus

....

4. Casey Affleck → Jennifer Garner

....

3 CONVERSATION *Asking about families*

A ▶ Listen and practice.

Rita: Tell me about your brother and sister, Sue.
Sue: Well, my sister works for the government.
Rita: Oh, what does she do?
Sue: I'm not sure. She's working on a very secret project right now.
Rita: Wow! And what about your brother?
Sue: He's a wildlife photographer.
Rita: What an interesting family! Can I meet them?
Sue: Sure, but not now. My sister's away. She's not working in the United States this month.
Rita: And your brother?
Sue: He's traveling in the Amazon.

B ▶ Listen to the rest of the conversation. Where do Rita's parents live? What do they do?

4 PRONUNCIATION *Intonation in statements*

A ▶ Listen and practice. Notice that statements usually have falling intonation.

He's traveling in the Amazon.   She's working on a very secret project.

B **PAIR WORK** Practice the conversation in Exercise 3 again. Pay attention to the intonation in the statements.

5 GRAMMAR FOCUS

Present continuous ▶

Are you **living** at home now?   Yes, I **am**.   No, I**'m not**.
Is your sister **working** for the government?   Yes, she **is**.   No, she**'s not**./No, she **isn't**.
Are Ed and Jill **taking** classes this year?   Yes, they **are**.   No, they**'re not**./No, they **aren't**.

Where **are** you **working** now?   I**'m not working**. I need a job.
What **is** your brother **doing**?   He**'s traveling** in the Amazon.
What **are** your friends **doing** these days?   They**'re studying** for their exams.

A Complete these phone conversations using the present continuous.

A: Hi, Stephanie. What .... you
.... (do)?
B: Hey, Mark. I .... (stand) in an
elevator, and it's stuck!
A: Oh, no! Are you OK?
B: Yeah. I – wait! It .... (move)
now. Thank goodness!

A: Marci, how .... you and Justin
.... (enjoy) your shopping trip?
B: We .... (have) a lot of fun.
A: .... your brother
.... (spend) a lot of money?
B: No, Mom. He .... (buy) only
one or two things. That's all!

B **PAIR WORK** Practice the phone conversations with a partner.

6 DISCUSSION *Is anyone . . . ?*

GROUP WORK Ask your classmates about people in their families. What are
they doing? Ask follow-up questions to get more information.

A: Is anyone in your family traveling right now?
B: Yes, my dad is. He's in South Korea.
C: What's he doing there?

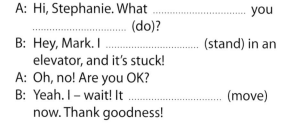

topics to ask about	
traveling	going to high school or college
living abroad	moving to a new home
taking a class	studying a foreign language

7 **INTERCHANGE 5** *Family facts*

Find out about your classmates' families. Go to Interchange 5 on page 119.

8 **SNAPSHOT**

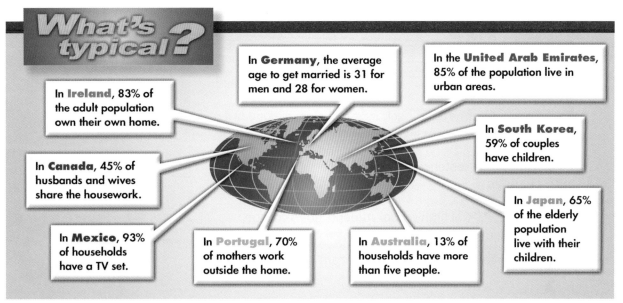

What's typical?

In **Ireland**, 83% of the adult population own their own home.

In **Germany**, the average age to get married is 31 for men and 28 for women.

In the **United Arab Emirates**, 85% of the population live in urban areas.

In **Canada**, 45% of husbands and wives share the housework.

In **South Korea**, 59% of couples have children.

In **Mexico**, 93% of households have a TV set.

In **Portugal**, 70% of mothers work outside the home.

In **Australia**, 13% of households have more than five people.

In **Japan**, 65% of the elderly population live with their children.

Source: nationmaster.com

Which facts surprise you? Why?
Which facts seem like positive things? Which seem negative?
How do you think your country compares?

9 **CONVERSATION** *Is that typical?*

A ▶ Listen and practice.

Marcos: How many brothers and sisters do you have, Mei-li?
Mei-li: Actually, I'm an only child.
Marcos: Really?
Mei-li: Yeah, a lot of families in China have only one child these days.
Marcos: I didn't know that.
Mei-li: What about you, Marcos?
Marcos: I come from a big family. I have three brothers and two sisters.
Mei-li: Wow! Is that typical in Peru?
Marcos: I'm not sure. Many families are smaller these days. But big families are great because you get a lot of birthday presents!

B ▶ Listen to the rest of the conversation.
What does Mei-li like about being an only child?

I come from a big family. ▪ 33

Quantifiers ▶

100%	All Nearly all Most	families have only one child.
	Many A lot of Some	families are smaller these days.
	Not many Few	couples have more than one child.
0%	No one	gets married before the age of 18.

A Rewrite these sentences using quantifiers. Then compare with a partner.

1. In the U.S., 75% of high school students go to college.

....

2. Seven percent of the people in Brazil are age 65 or older.

....

3. In India, 0% of the people vote before the age of 18.

....

4. Forty percent of the people in Sweden live alone.

....

5. In Singapore, 23% of the people speak English at home.

....

B **PAIR WORK** Rewrite the sentences in part A so that they are true about your country.

> In . . . , many high school students go to college.

11 *WRITING* *An email about your family*

A Write an email to your e-pal about your family.

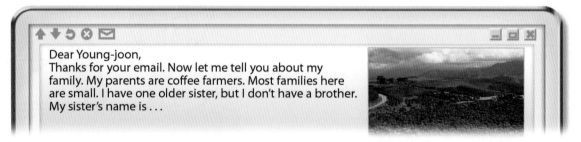

Dear Young-joon,
Thanks for your email. Now let me tell you about my family. My parents are coffee farmers. Most families here are small. I have one older sister, but I don't have a brother. My sister's name is . . .

B **GROUP WORK** Take turns reading your emails. Ask questions to get more information.

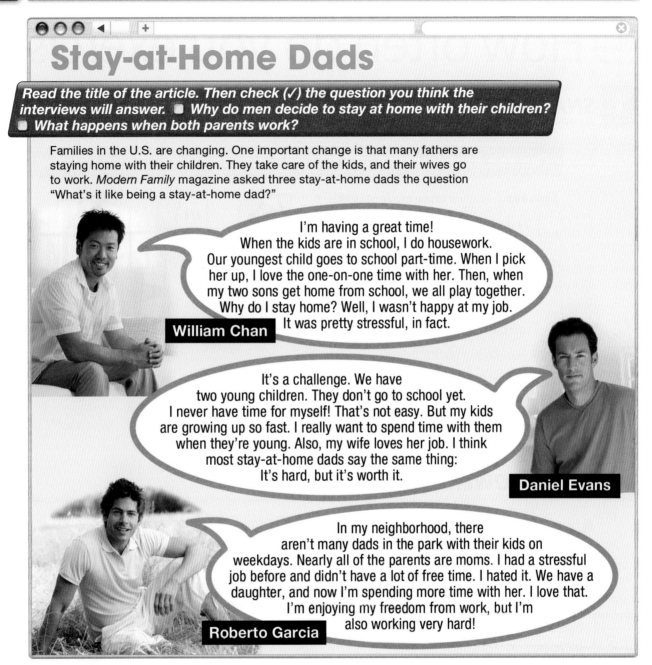

Stay-at-Home Dads

Read the title of the article. Then check (✓) the question you think the interviews will answer. ☐ **Why do men decide to stay at home with their children?** ☐ **What happens when both parents work?**

Families in the U.S. are changing. One important change is that many fathers are staying home with their children. They take care of the kids, and their wives go to work. *Modern Family* magazine asked three stay-at-home dads the question "What's it like being a stay-at-home dad?"

William Chan

I'm having a great time! When the kids are in school, I do housework. Our youngest child goes to school part-time. When I pick her up, I love the one-on-one time with her. Then, when my two sons get home from school, we all play together. Why do I stay home? Well, I wasn't happy at my job. It was pretty stressful, in fact.

Daniel Evans

It's a challenge. We have two young children. They don't go to school yet. I never have time for myself! That's not easy. But my kids are growing up so fast. I really want to spend time with them when they're young. Also, my wife loves her job. I think most stay-at-home dads say the same thing: It's hard, but it's worth it.

Roberto Garcia

In my neighborhood, there aren't many dads in the park with their kids on weekdays. Nearly all of the parents are moms. I had a stressful job before and didn't have a lot of free time. I hated it. We have a daughter, and now I'm spending more time with her. I love that. I'm enjoying my freedom from work, but I'm also working very hard!

A Read the interviews. Check (✓) the correct names.

Who . . . ?	William	Daniel	Roberto
1. has more than two children	☐	☐	☐
2. has an only child	☐	☐	☐
3. had a stressful career	☐	☐	☐
4. thinks it's hard to stay at home	☐	☐	☐
5. has a wife with a great job	☐	☐	☐

B PAIR WORK What do the dads like about staying at home? What challenges are they having? What are some other reasons dads stay at home?

6 How often do you exercise?

1 SNAPSHOT

The Top Five Sports and Fitness Activities in the United States

Sports
- basketball
- baseball
- soccer
- football
- softball

Fitness Activities
- walking
- weight training
- treadmill
- stretching
- jogging

Source: SGMA International, *Sports Participation in America*

Do people in your country enjoy any of these sports or activities?
Check (✓) the sports or fitness activities you enjoy.
Make a list of other sports or activities you do. Then compare with the class.

2 WORD POWER *Sports and exercise*

A Which of these activities are popular with the following age groups?
Check (✓) the activities. Then compare with a partner.

	Children	Teens	Young adults	Middle-aged people	Older people
aerobics	☐	☐	☐	☐	☐
bicycling	☐	☐	☐	☐	☐
bowling	☐	☐	☐	☐	☐
golf	☐	☐	☐	☐	☐
karate	☐	☐	☐	☐	☐
swimming	☐	☐	☐	☐	☐
tennis	☐	☐	☐	☐	☐
volleyball	☐	☐	☐	☐	☐
yoga	☐	☐	☐	☐	☐

B **PAIR WORK** Which activities in part A are used with *do*, *go*, or *play*?

do aerobics .... go bicycling .... play golf ....

....

....

3 **CONVERSATION** *I hardly ever exercise.*

A ▶ Listen and practice.

Marie: You're really fit, Paul. Do you exercise a lot?
Paul: Well, I almost always get up early, and I lift weights for an hour.
Marie: Seriously?
Paul: Sure. And then I often go swimming.
Marie: Wow! How often do you exercise like that?
Paul: About five times a week. What about you?
Marie: Oh, I hardly ever exercise. I usually just watch TV in my free time. I guess I'm a real couch potato!

B ▶ Listen to the rest of the conversation. What else does Paul do in his free time?

4 **GRAMMAR FOCUS**

Adverbs of frequency ▶

How often do you exercise?	Do you **ever** watch TV in the evening?	100%	**always**
I lift weights **every day**.	Yes, I **often** watch TV after dinner.		**almost always**
I go jogging **once a week**.	I **sometimes** watch TV before bed.		**usually**
I play soccer **twice a month**.	**Sometimes** I watch TV before bed.*		**often**
I swim about **three times a year**.	I **hardly ever** watch TV.		**sometimes**
I don't exercise very **often/much**.	No, I **never** watch TV.		**hardly ever**
Usually I exercise before work.*			**almost never**
	*__Usually__ and **sometimes** can begin a sentence.	0%	**never**

A Put the adverbs in the correct place. Then practice with a partner.

1. A: Do you play sports? (ever)
   B: Sure. I play soccer. (twice a week)

2. A: What do you do on Saturday mornings? (usually)
   B: Nothing much. I sleep until noon. (almost always)

3. A: Do you do aerobics at the gym? (often)
   B: No, I do aerobics. (hardly ever)

4. A: Do you exercise on Sundays? (always)
   B: No, I exercise on Sundays. (never)

5. A: What do you do after class? (usually)
   B: I go out with my classmates. (about three times a week)

B **PAIR WORK** Take turns asking the questions in part A. Give your own information when answering.

PRONUNCIATION *Intonation with direct address*

A ▶ Listen and practice. Notice these statements with direct address.
There is usually falling intonation and a pause before the name.

You're really fit, Paul.   You look tired, Marie.   I feel great, Dr. Lee.

B **PAIR WORK** Write four statements using direct address.
Then practice them.

 SPEAKING *Fitness poll*

A **GROUP WORK** Take a poll in your group. One person takes notes.
Take turns asking each person these questions.

1. Do you have a regular fitness program? How often do you exercise?

2. Do you ever go to a gym? How often do you go? What do you do there?

3. Do you play any sports? Which ones? How often do you play them?

4. Do you ever take long walks? How often? Where do you go?

5. What else do you do to keep fit?

B **GROUP WORK** Study the results of the poll. Who in your group
has a good fitness program?

7 **LISTENING** *In the evening*

A ▶ Listen to three people discuss what they like to do in the evening.
Complete the chart.

	Activity	How often?
Justin	....	....
Carrie	....	....
Marcos	....	....

B ▶ Listen again. Who is most similar to you – Justin, Carrie, or Marcos?

8 DISCUSSION *Sports and athletes*

GROUP WORK Take turns asking and answering these questions.

Who's your favorite male athlete? Why?
Who's your favorite female athlete? Why?
Who are three famous athletes in your country?
What's your favorite sports team? Why?
Do you ever watch sports on TV? Which ones?
Do you ever watch sports live? Which ones?
What are two sports you don't like?
What sport or activity do you want to try?

9 WRITING *About favorite activities*

A Write about your favorite activities. Include one activity that is false.

> I love to exercise! I usually work out every day. I get up early in the morning and go jogging for about 30 minutes. Then I often go to the gym and do yoga. Sometimes I play tennis in the afternoon. I play . . .

B **GROUP WORK** Take turns reading your descriptions. Can you guess the false information?

"You don't play tennis in the afternoon. Right?"

10 CONVERSATION *I'm a real fitness freak.*

A Listen and practice.

Ruth: You're in great shape, Keith.
Keith: Thanks. I guess I'm a real fitness freak.
Ruth: How often do you work out?
Keith: Well, I do aerobics twice a week. And I play tennis every week.
Ruth: Tennis? That sounds like a lot of fun.
Keith: Oh, do you want to play sometime?
Ruth: Uh, . . . how well do you play?
Keith: Pretty well, I guess.
Ruth: Well, all right. But I'm not very good.
Keith: No problem. I'll give you a few tips.

B Listen to Keith and Ruth after their tennis match. Who's the winner?

11 GRAMMAR FOCUS

Questions with how; short answers ▶

How often do you work out?	**How well** do you play tennis?
Every day.	**Pretty well.**
Twice a week.	**About average.**
Not very often.	**Not very well.**
How long do you spend at the gym?	**How good** are you at sports?
Thirty minutes a day.	**Pretty good.**
Two hours a week.	**OK.**
About an hour on weekends.	**Not so good.**

A Complete these questions. Then practice with a partner.

1. A: .... at volleyball?
   B: I guess I'm pretty good. I often play on weekends.

2. A: .... spend online?
   B: About an hour after dinner. I like to chat with my friends.

3. A: .... play chess?
   B: Once or twice a month. It's a good way to relax.

4. A: .... swim?
   B: Not very well. I need to take swimming lessons.

B GROUP WORK Take turns asking the questions in part A. Give your own information when answering.

12 LISTENING I'm terrible at sports.

▶ Listen to Dan, Jean, Sally, and Phil discuss sports and exercise. Who is a couch potato? a fitness freak? a sports nut? a gym rat?

a couch potato	**a fitness freak**	**a sports nut**	**a gym rat**
1.	2.	3.	4. ....

13 INTERCHANGE 6 Do you dance?

Find out what your classmates can do. Go to Interchange 6 on page 120.

Health and Fitness Quiz

How healthy and fit do you think you are? Skim the questions below.
Then guess your health and fitness score from 0 (very unhealthy) to 50 (very healthy).

Your Food and Nutrition

1. How many meals do you eat each day?   Points
- Four or five small meals   5
- Three meals   3
- One or two big meals   0

2. How often do you eat at regular times during the day?
- Almost always   5
- Usually   3
- Hardly ever   0

3. How many servings of fruits or vegetables do you eat each day?
- Five or more   5
- One to four   3
- None   0

4. How much junk food do you eat?
- Very little   5
- About average   3
- A lot   0

5. Do you take vitamins?
- Yes, every day   5
- Sometimes   3
- No   0

Your Fitness

6. How often do you exercise or play a sport?   Points
- Three or more days a week   5
- One or two days a week   3
- Never   0

7. Which best describes your exercise program?   Points
- Both weight training and aerobic exercise   5
- Either weight training or aerobic exercise   3
- None   0

8. How important is your fitness program to you?
- Very important   5
- Fairly important   3
- Not very important   0

Your Health

9. How often do you get a physical exam?   Points
- Once a year   5
- Every two or three years   3
- Rarely   0

10. How often do you sleep well?
- Always   5
- Usually or sometimes   3
- Hardly ever or never   0

Rate yourself

TOTAL POINTS

42 to 50: Excellent job! Keep up the good work!

28 to 41: Good! Your health and fitness are above average.

15 to 27: Your health and fitness are a little below average.

14 or below: You can improve your health and fitness.

A Take the quiz and add up your score. Is your score similar to your original guess? Do you agree with your quiz score? Why or why not?

B GROUP WORK Compare your scores. Who is the healthiest and fittest? What can you do to improve your health and fitness?

Units 5-6 Progress check

SELF-ASSESSMENT

How well can you do these things? Check (✓) the boxes.

I can	Very well	OK	A little
Ask about and describe present activities (Ex. 1, 2, 3)	☐	☐	☐
Describe family life (Ex. 3)	☐	☐	☐
Ask for and give personal information (Ex. 3)	☐	☐	☐
Give information about quantities (Ex. 3)	☐	☐	☐
Ask and answer questions about free time (Ex. 4)	☐	☐	☐
Ask and answer questions about routines and abilities (Ex. 4)	☐	☐	☐

1 LISTENING *What are they doing?*

A ▶ Listen to people do different things. What are they doing? Complete the chart.

B PAIR WORK Compare your answers.

A: In number one, someone is watching TV.
B: I don't think so. I think someone is . . .

What are they doing?
1. ....
2. ....
3. ....
4. ....

2 GAME *Memory test*

GROUP WORK Choose a person in the room, but don't say who! Other students ask yes/no questions to guess the person.

A: I'm thinking of someone in the classroom.
B: Is it a woman?
A: Yes, it is.
C: Is she sitting in the front of the room?
A: No, she isn't.
D: Is she sitting in the back?
A: Yes, she is.
E: Is she wearing jeans?
A: No, she isn't.
B: Is it . . . ?

The student with the correct guess has the next turn.

3 SURVEY Family life

A **GROUP WORK** Add two more yes/no questions about family life to the chart. Then ask and answer the questions in groups. Write down the number of "yes" and "no" answers. (Remember to include yourself.)

	Number of "yes" answers	Number of "no" answers
1. Are you living with your family?	....	....
2. Do your parents both work?	....	....
3. Do you eat dinner with your family?	....	....
4. Are you working these days?	....	....
5. Are you married?	....	....
6. Do you have any children?	....	....
7.	....	....
8.	....	....

B **GROUP WORK** Write up the results of the survey. Then tell the class.

> 1. In our group, most people are living with their family.
> 2. Few of our parents both work.

4 DISCUSSION Routines and abilities

GROUP WORK Choose three questions. Then ask your questions in groups. When someone answers "yes," think of other questions to ask.

Do you ever . . . ?
- [ ] sing karaoke
- [ ] listen to English songs
- [ ] chat online
- [ ] do weight training
- [ ] play golf
- [ ] play video games
- [ ] cook for friends
- [ ] go swimming
- [ ] watch old movies

A: **Do you ever** sing karaoke?
B: Yes, I often do.
C: **What** song do you like to sing?
B: "I Love Rock 'n' Roll."
A: **When** do you sing karaoke?
B: In the evenings.
C: **How often** do you go?
B: Every weekend!
D: **How well** do you sing?
B: Not very well. But I have a lot of fun!

WHAT'S NEXT?

Look at your Self-assessment again. Do you need to review anything?

7 We had a great time!

SNAPSHOT

The Top Eight Leisure-Time Activities in the United States

☐ read ☐ watch TV ☐ spend time with family ☐ play sports

☐ go to the gym ☐ use the computer ☐ go fishing ☐ go to the movies

Source: The Harris Poll

Check (✓) the activities you do in your free time.
List three other activities you do in your free time.
What are your favorite leisure-time activities?

2 **CONVERSATION** *Did you do anything special?*

A ▶ Listen and practice.

Rick: So, what did you do last weekend, Meg?
Meg: Oh, I had a great time. I went to a karaoke bar and sang with some friends on Saturday.
Rick: How fun! Did you go to Lucky's?
Meg: No, we didn't. We went to that new place downtown. How about you? Did you go anywhere?
Rick: No, I didn't go anywhere all weekend. I just stayed home and studied for today's Spanish test.
Meg: Our test is today? I forgot about that!
Rick: Don't worry. You always get an A.

B ▶ Listen to the rest of the conversation.
What does Meg do on Sunday afternoons?

Simple past ▶

Did you **work** on Saturday?
    Yes, I **did**. I **worked** all day.
    No, I **didn't**. I **didn't work** at all.

Did you **go** anywhere last weekend?
    Yes, I **did**. I **went** to the movies.
    No, I **didn't**. I **didn't go** anywhere.

What **did** Rick **do** on Saturday?
He **stayed** home and **studied** for a test.

How **did** Meg **spend** her weekend?
She **went** to a karaoke bar and **sang**
    with some friends.

A Complete these conversations. Then practice with a partner.

1. A: .... you .... (stay) home on Saturday?
  B: No, I .... (call) my friend. We .... (drive)
    to a café for lunch.
2. A: How .... you .... (spend) your last birthday?
  B: I .... (have) a party. Everyone .... (enjoy) it,
    but the neighbors .... (not, like) the noise.
3. A: What .... you .... (do) last night?
  B: I .... (see) a 3-D movie at the Cineplex.
    I .... (love) it!
4. A: .... you .... (do) anything special over the weekend?
  B: Yes, I .... I .... (go) shopping. Unfortunately,
    I .... (spend) all my money. Now I'm broke!
5. A: .... you .... (go) out on Friday night?
  B: No, I .... I .... (invite) friends over,
    and I .... (cook) dinner for them.

regular verbs	
work	→ worked
invite	→ invited
study	→ studied
stop	→ stopped

irregular verbs	
do	→ **did**
drive	→ **drove**
have	→ **had**
go	→ **went**
sing	→ **sang**
see	→ **saw**
spend	→ **spent**

B **PAIR WORK** Take turns asking the questions in part A.
Give your own information when answering.

A: Did you stay home on Saturday?
B: No, I didn't. I went out with some friends.

4 *PRONUNCIATION* Reduction of did you

A ▶ Listen and practice. Notice how **did you** is reduced in the
following questions.

[dɪdʒə]
Did you have a good time?

[wədɪdʒə]
What did you do last night?

[haʊdɪdʒə]
How did you like the movie?

B **PAIR WORK** Practice the questions in Exercise 3, part A again.
Pay attention to the pronunciation of **did you**.

5 **WORD POWER** *Chores and activities*

A Find two other words or phrases from the list that usually
go with each verb.

a lot of fun	dancing	a good time	shopping	a vacation
the bed	the dishes	the laundry	a trip	a video

do	my homework	....	....
go	online	....	....
have	a party	....	....
make	a phone call	....	....
take	a day off	....	....

B Circle the things you did last weekend. Then compare with a partner.

A: I went shopping with my friends. We had a good time.
B: I didn't have a very good time. I did the laundry and . . .

6 **DISCUSSION** *Any questions?*

GROUP WORK Take turns. One student
makes a statement about the weekend.
Other students ask questions. Each
student answers at least three questions.

A: I went dancing on Saturday night.
B: **Where** did you go?
A: To the Rock-it Club.
C: **Who** did you go with?
A: I went with my friends.
D: **What time** did you go?
A: We went around 10:00.

7 **LISTENING** *What did you do last night?*

A Listen to John and Laura
describe what they did last night.
Check (✓) the correct information
about each person.

Who . . . ?	John	Laura
went to a party	☐	☐
had a good meal	☐	☐
watched a video	☐	☐
met an old friend	☐	☐
got home late	☐	☐

B Listen again. Who had a
good time? Who didn't have a
good time? Why or why not?

INTERCHANGE 7 *Thinking back*

Play a board game. Go to Interchange 7 on page 121.

9 **CONVERSATION** *How was your vacation?*

A ▶ Listen and practice.

Celia: Hi, Don. How was your vacation?
Don: It was excellent! I went to Hawaii with my cousin. We had a great time.
Celia: Lucky you. How long were you there?
Don: About a week.
Celia: Fantastic! Was the weather OK?
Don: Not really. It was cloudy a lot. But we went surfing every day. The waves were amazing.
Celia: So, what was the best thing about the trip?
Don: Well, something incredible happened. . . .

B ▶ Listen to the rest of the conversation. What happened?

10 **GRAMMAR FOCUS**

> **Past of be** ▶
>
> | | | **Contractions** |
> |---|---|---|
> | **Were** you in Hawaii? | Yes, I **was**. | was**n't** = was not |
> | **Was** the weather OK? | No, it **wasn't**. | were**n't** = were not |
> | **Were** you and your cousin on vacation? | Yes, we **were**. | |
> | **Were** your parents there? | No, they **weren't**. | |
> | How long **were** you away? | I **was** away for a week. | |
> | How **was** your vacation? | It **was** excellent! | |

Complete these conversations. Then practice with a partner.

1. A: .... you in Los Angeles last weekend?
   B: No, I .... I .... in San Francisco.
   A: How .... it?
   B: It .... great! But it .... foggy and cool as usual.

2. A: How long .... your parents in Europe?
   B: They .... there for two weeks.
   A: .... they in London the whole time?
   B: No, they .... They also went to Paris.

3. A: .... you away last week?
   B: Yes, I .... in Istanbul.
   A: Really? How long .... you there?
   B: For almost a week. I .... there on business.

Golden Gate Bridge

11 DISCUSSION On vacation

A **GROUP WORK** Ask your classmates about their last vacations.
Ask these questions or your own ideas.

Where did you spend your last vacation?   What did you do?
How long was your vacation?   How was the weather?
Who were you with?   What would you like to do on your next vacation?

B **CLASS ACTIVITY** Who had an interesting vacation? Tell the class who and why.

12 WRITING An online post

A Read this online post.

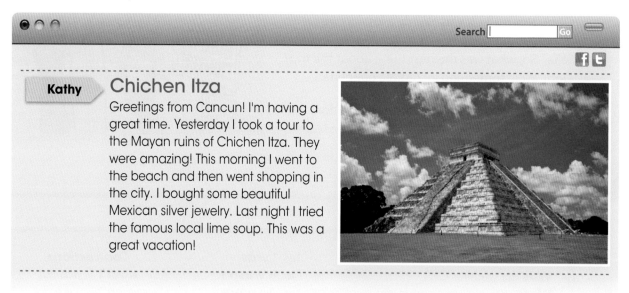

Search [   ] [Go]

Kathy

Chichen Itza

Greetings from Cancun! I'm having a great time. Yesterday I took a tour to the Mayan ruins of Chichen Itza. They were amazing! This morning I went to the beach and then went shopping in the city. I bought some beautiful Mexican silver jewelry. Last night I tried the famous local lime soup. This was a great vacation!

B Write an online post to a partner about your last vacation. Then exchange messages. Do you have any questions about the vacation?

13 LISTENING Welcome back.

A ▶ Listen to Jason and Barbara talk about their vacations.
Write where they went and what they did there.

	Where they went	What they did	Did they enjoy it?	
			Yes	No
Jason	....	....	☐	☐
Barbara	....	....	☐	☐

B ▶ Listen again. Did they enjoy their vacations? Check (✓) Yes or No.

Look at the pictures. What do you think each person did on his or her vacation?

Search [   ] Go

Rachel ▶ **Terracotta Warriors**

I arrived in China two weeks ago, but my trip is almost over! I'm with a group from the university. We stayed with families in Beijing for a week. We studied Mandarin every day, and I practiced a lot with my host family. Then my group took a trip to Xi'an. We saw the terracotta statues and learned about Chinese history. I'm tired, but I loved every minute of my trip.

1

Hee-jin ▶ **Sanibel Island, Florida**

I just spent a week at a yoga retreat in Florida. Every day, I did yoga, went for long walks on the beach, collected seashells, and ate great vegetarian food. I also learned how to play tennis. I feel fantastic! Now I'm going to visit friends in Miami for a few days. Click on my photo album to see more pictures!

2

Chris ▶ **Greetings from Chile**

Chile is amazing! I just returned from a trip to the Torres del Paine National Park. We took a plane to a boat to a bus to get to the park. I was with four other friends. We camped outside and hiked around the park for 10 days. I saw glaciers and lots of wildlife, including some pink flamingos. Now I'm back in Santiago for a week.

3

A Read the online posts. Then write the number of the post where each sentence could go.

.... It was a long trip, but I was so happy after we got there!
.... I really recommend this place – it's very relaxing.
.... I had a great trip, but now I need a vacation!

B **PAIR WORK** Answer these questions.

1. Which person had a fitness vacation?
2. Who learned a lot on vacation?
3. Who had a vacation that was full of adventure?
4. Which vacation sounds the most interesting to you? Why?

What's your neighborhood like?

1 WORD POWER *Places*

A Match the words and the definitions. Then ask and answer the questions with a partner.

What's a . . . ?   *It's a place where you . . .*

1. barbershop ....   a. wash and dry clothes
2. grocery store ....   b. buy food
3. laundromat ....   c. buy cards and paper
4. library ....   d. get a haircut
5. stationery store ....   e. see a movie or play
6. theater ....   f. make reservations for a trip
7. travel agency ....   g. borrow books

B **PAIR WORK** Write definitions for these places.

clothing store   drugstore   Internet café   music store   post office

It's a place where you find new fashions. (clothing store)

C **GROUP WORK** Read your definitions. Can others guess the places?

2 CONVERSATION *I'm your new neighbor.*

Listen and practice.

Jack: Excuse me. I'm your new neighbor, Jack.
           I just moved in.
Mrs. Day: Oh. Yes?
Jack: I'm looking for a grocery store. Are there
           any around here?
Mrs. Day: Yes, there are some on Pine Street.
Jack: Oh, good. And is there a laundromat
           near here?
Mrs. Day: Well, I think there's one across from the
           shopping center.
Jack: Thank you.
Mrs. Day: By the way, there's a barbershop in the
           shopping center, too.
Jack: A barbershop?

There is, there are; one, any, some ▶

Is there a laundromat near here? 　Yes, **there is**. There's **one** across from the shopping center. 　No, **there isn't**, but there's **one** next to the library. **Are there any** grocery stores around here? 　Yes, **there are**. There are **some** nice stores on Pine Street. 　No, **there aren't**, but there are **some** on Third Avenue. 　No, **there aren't any** around here.	**Prepositions** on next to near/close to across from/opposite in front of in back of/behind between on the corner of

A Look at the map below. Write questions about these places.

a bank	an electronics store	grocery stores	hotels	a post office
a department store	gas stations	a gym	a pay phone	restaurants

> Is there a bank around here?
>
> Are there any gas stations on Main Street?

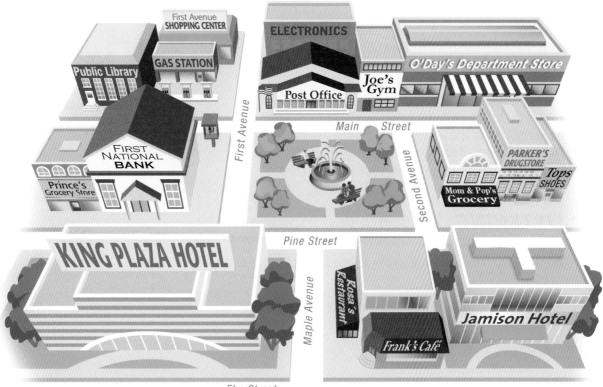

B **PAIR WORK** Ask and answer the questions you wrote in part A.

A: Is there a pay phone around here?
B: Yes, there is. There's one across from the gas station.

4 PRONUNCIATION *Reduction of there is/there are*

A ▶ Listen and practice. Notice how **there is** and **there are** are reduced in conversation, except for short answers.

Is there a laundromat near here?
    Yes, **there is**. **There's** one across from the shopping center.

Are there any grocery stores around here?
    Yes, **there are**. **There are** some on Pine Street.

B Practice the questions and answers in Exercise 3, part B again.

5 SPEAKING *My neighborhood*

GROUP WORK Take turns asking and answering questions about places like these in your neighborhood.

a bookstore	an Internet café
coffee shops	a karaoke bar
dance clubs	a library
drugstores	movie theaters
an electronics store	a park
a gym	restaurants

A: Is there a good bookstore in your neighborhood?
B: Yes, there's an excellent one across from the park.
C: Are there any coffee shops?
B: Sorry, I don't know.
D: Are there any cool dance clubs?
B: I'm not sure, but I think there's one . . .

useful expressions
Sorry, I don't know.
I'm not sure, but I think . . .
Of course. There's one . . .

6 LISTENING *What are you looking for?*

A ▶ Listen to hotel guests ask about places to visit. Complete the chart.

Place	Location	Interesting?	
		Yes	No
Hard Rock Cafe	....	☐	☐
Science Museum	....	☐	☐
Aquarium	....	☐	☐

B **PAIR WORK** Which place sounds the most interesting to you? Why?

7 SNAPSHOT

Common Complaints About Neighbors

Noise

☐ "My neighbor's dog barks all night."
☐ "My neighbor always listens to loud music."

Cleanliness

☐ "My neighbor puts his garbage in the hall."
☐ "There are always shoes outside my door."

Pets

☐ "My neighbor's cats go everywhere."
☐ "My neighbor has six dogs. It's like a zoo!"

Privacy

☐ "My neighbor's kids visit every day. It's too much!"
☐ "My neighbor always asks me for things."

Source: Based on information from njcooperator.com

Check (✓) the complaints you have about your neighbors.
What other complaints do you have about neighbors?
What do you do when you have complaints?

8 CONVERSATION *It's pretty safe.*

▶ Listen and practice.

Nick: How do you like your new apartment?
Pam: I love it. It's downtown, so it's very convenient.
Nick: Downtown? Is there much noise?
Pam: No, there isn't any. I live on the fifth floor.
Nick: How many restaurants are there near your place?
Pam: A lot. In fact, there's an excellent Korean place just around the corner.
Nick: What about parking?
Pam: Well, there aren't many parking garages. But I usually find a place on the street.
Nick: Is there much crime?
Pam: No, it's pretty safe. Hold on. That's my car alarm! I'll call you back later.

GRAMMAR FOCUS

Quantifiers; how many *and* how much ▶

Count nouns	Noncount nouns
Are there **many restaurants**?	Is there **much crime**?
Yes, there are **a lot**.	Yes, there's **a lot**.
Yes, there are **a few**.	Yes, there's **a little**.
No, there are**n't many**.	No, there is**n't much**.
No, there are**n't any**.	No, there is**n't any**.
No, there are **none**.	No, there's **none**.
How many restaurants are there?	**How much** crime is there?
There are ten or twelve.	There's a lot of street crime.

A Write answers to these questions about your neighborhood. Then practice with a partner.

1. Is there much parking? ....
2. Are there many apartment buildings? ....
3. How much traffic is there? ....
4. How many dance clubs are there? ....
5. Is there much noise? ....
6. Are there many pay phones? ....
7. Is there much pollution? ....
8. How many swimming pools are there? ....

B GROUP WORK Write questions like those in part A about these topics. Then ask and answer the questions.

cafés   crime   parks   pollution   public transportation   schools   traffic lights

 INTERCHANGE 8 *Where am I?*

Play a guessing game. Go to Interchange 8 on page 122.

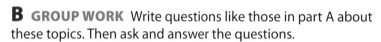 **WRITING** *A "roommate wanted" ad*

A Read these ads asking for roommates.

B Now write a "roommate wanted" ad. Use your real name at the end, but you can use a false phone number or email address.

C CLASS ACTIVITY Put your ads on the wall. Read the ads and choose one. Then find the person who wrote it. Ask questions to get more information.

Roommates 🏠 Wanted

Roommate needed to share large 3-bedroom apt. in nice neighborhood. Great park across the street. Only $440 a month! Parking available. Call Sheri or Jen at 352-555-8381.

Quiet student looking for roommate to share 2-bedroom house near university. Near public transportation. Pets OK. $550 a month plus utilities. Email Greg at g.adams@cup.com.

The World in One Neighborhood

Scan the article. Then check (✓) the countries that are not mentioned.
■ Brazil ■ China ■ Greece ■ India ■ Spain ■ Sudan ■ Uruguay ■ Vietnam

1 The sidewalks are crowded with people chatting in Cantonese. An Indian man sells spices from his corner shop. Brazilian music plays loudly from a café. Is it China? India? Brazil? No, it's Kensington Market, a neighborhood in Toronto, Canada. Kensington Market was once an Eastern European and Italian neighborhood, but the area changed along with its residents. First came the Portuguese, then East Asians, then people from Iran, Vietnam, Sudan, Brazil, the Caribbean, and the Middle East.

2 Today, the neighborhood is truly multicultural – you can hear more than 100 languages on its streets. New residents bring many new traditions. "What's really cool about Kensington is that as soon as you're in it, you feel as though you're not in Toronto anymore," says one resident. "I think what makes Kensington Market unique is that it's always changing," says another.

3 It isn't surprising that the area in and around Kensington Market is becoming a popular place to live. The rents are reasonable, the neighborhood is exciting, and it has good public transportation. There are apartments of every size and for every budget. It has inexpensive stores, fun cafés, fresh fruit and vegetable markets, and restaurants with almost every type of cuisine. As one resident says, "This place is the heart of Toronto."

A Read the article. Then write the number of each paragraph next to its main idea.

.... The residents and their traditions make Kensington Market a multicultural neighborhood.
.... People from all over the world live in Kensington Market.
.... The neighborhood has many good characteristics.

B Check (✓) the things you can find in Kensington Market.

◻ inexpensive stores   ◻ beautiful beaches   ◻ many different cultures
◻ big apartments   ◻ great markets   ◻ interesting old buildings
◻ good schools   ◻ good restaurants   ◻ good public transportation

C PAIR WORK Do you know of a neighborhood that is similar to Kensington Market? Describe it.

Units 7–8 Progress check

SELF-ASSESSMENT

How well can you do these things? Check (✓) the boxes.

I can	Very well	OK	A little
Understand descriptions of past events (Ex. 1)	☐	☐	☐
Describe events in the past (Ex. 1)	☐	☐	☐
Ask and answer questions about past activities (Ex. 2)	☐	☐	☐
Give and understand simple directions (Ex. 3)	☐	☐	☐
Talk about my neighborhood (Ex. 4)	☐	☐	☐

1 LISTENING *Frankie's weekend*

A ▶ A thief robbed a house on Saturday. A detective is questioning Frankie. The pictures show what Frankie really did on Saturday. Listen to their conversation. Are Frankie's answers true (**T**) or false (**F**)?

1:00 P.M. T F   3:00 P.M. T F   5:00 P.M. T F   6:00 P.M. T F   8:00 P.M. T F   10:30 P.M. T F

B PAIR WORK What did Frankie really do? Use the pictures to retell the story.

2 DISCUSSION *What do you remember?*

A Do you remember what you did yesterday? Check (✓) the things you did. Then add two other things you did.

☐ got up early   ☐ went shopping   ☐ did the dishes   ☐ went to bed late
☐ went to class   ☐ ate at a restaurant   ☐ watched TV   ☐ ....
☐ made phone calls   ☐ did the laundry   ☐ exercised   ☐ ....

B GROUP WORK Ask questions about each thing in part A.

A: Did you get up early yesterday?
B: No, I didn't. I got up at 10:00. I was very tired.

3 SPEAKING *The neighborhood*

A Create a neighborhood. Add five places to "My map." Choose from this list.

a bank   cafés   a dance club   a drugstore   gas stations   a gym   a theater

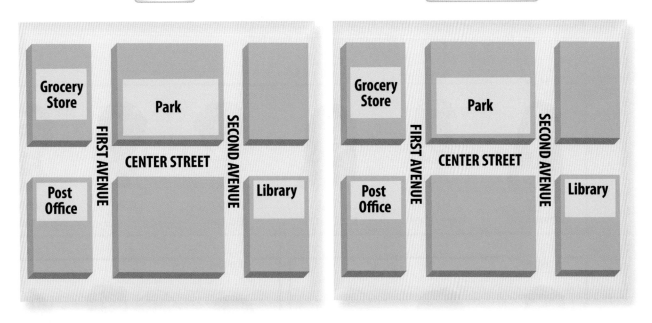

B PAIR WORK Ask questions about your partner's map. (But don't look!) Draw the places on "My partner's map." Then compare your maps.

A: Are there any cafés in the neighborhood?
B: Yes, there's one on the corner of Center Street and First Avenue.

4 ROLE PLAY *What's it like?*

Student A: Imagine you are a visitor in Student B's neighborhood. Ask questions about it.
Student B: Imagine a visitor wants to find out about your neighborhood. Answer the visitor's questions.

    A: How much crime is there?
    B: There isn't much. It's a very safe neighborhood.
    A: Is there much noise?
    B: Well, yes, there's a lot. . . .

Change roles and try the role play again.

topics to ask about
crime
noise
parks
places to shop
pollution
public transportation
schools
traffic

WHAT'S NEXT?

Look at your Self-assessment again. Do you need to review anything?

What does she look like?

1 WORD POWER *Appearance*

A Look at these expressions. What are three more words or expressions to describe people? Write them in the box below.

Hair

long brown hair | short blond hair | straight black hair | curly red hair | bald | a mustache and beard

Age

young | middle-aged | elderly

Looks

handsome | good-looking | pretty

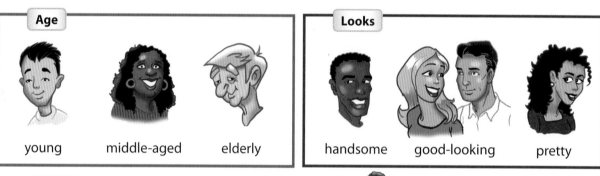

Height

short | fairly short | medium height | pretty tall | very tall

Other words or expressions

....
....
....

B PAIR WORK Choose at least four expressions to describe yourself and your partner. Then compare. Do you agree?

A: You have curly black hair. You're young and good-looking.
B: I don't agree. My hair isn't very curly.

Me	My partner
....	....
....	....
....	....
....	....

2 CONVERSATION *She's very tall.*

A ▶ Listen and practice.

Emily: I hear you have a new girlfriend, Randy.
Randy: Yes. Her name's Ashley, and she's
        gorgeous!
Emily: Really? What does she look like?
Randy: Well, she's very tall.
Emily: How tall?
Randy: About 6 feet 2, I suppose.
Emily: Wow, that *is* tall. What color is her hair?
Randy: She has beautiful red hair.
Emily: And how old is she?
Randy: I don't know. She won't tell me.

B ▶ Listen to the rest of the conversation.
What else do you learn about Ashley?

3 GRAMMAR FOCUS

Describing people ▶

General appearance	Age	Height	Hair

What does she look like?
  She's tall, with red hair.
  She's gorgeous.
	How old is she?
	  She's about 32.
	  She's in her thirties.
		How tall is she?
		  She's 1 meter 88.
		  She's 6 feet 2.
			How long is her hair?
			  It's medium length.

Does he wear glasses?
  Yes, and he has a beard.
	How old is he?
	  He's in his twenties.
		How tall is he?
		  He's pretty short.
			What color is his hair?
			  It's dark/light brown.
			  He has brown hair.

A Write questions to match these statements. Then compare with a partner.

1. .... ?   My brother is 26.
2. .... ?   I'm 173 cm (5 feet 8).
3. .... ?   My mother has brown hair.
4. .... ?   No, she wears contact lenses.
5. .... ?   He's tall and very good-looking.
6. .... ?   My sister's hair is medium length.
7. .... ?   I have dark brown eyes.

B **PAIR WORK** Choose a person in your class. Don't tell your partner who
it is. Your partner will ask questions to guess the person's name.

A: Is it a man or a woman?
B: It's a man.
A: How tall is he?
B: . . .

4 LISTENING *Who is it?*

A ▶ Listen to descriptions of six people. Number them from 1 to 6.

B ▶ Listen again. How old is each person?

5 INTERCHANGE 9 *Find the differences*

Compare two pictures of a party. Student A go to Interchange 9A on page 123. Student B go to Interchange 9B on page 124.

6 WRITING *An email describing people*

A Imagine your e-pal is coming to visit you for the first time. You and a classmate are meeting him or her at the airport. Write an email describing yourself and your classmate. (Don't give the classmate's name.)

Re: Your visit

Dear Hasma,
I'm meeting you at the airport at noon on Sunday.
My friend is coming with me. Attached is a photo of
both of us. As you can see, we're both in our late teens.
My friend is fairly tall and very pretty. She has . . .

B **GROUP WORK** Read your email to the group. Can they guess the classmate you are describing?

7 SNAPSHOT

FASHION on the STREET
Describe your style...

CLASSIC
— button-down shirt
— belt
— slacks
— dress shoes

COOL and casual
cap
— jacket
— cargo pants
— boots

FUNKY
— T-shirt
— purse
— plaid skirt
— striped tights
— sneakers

Source: Based on an idea from *Time Out New York*

Which clothing items do you often wear? Circle the items.
What are three more things you like to wear?
What's your style? Is it classic? cool and casual? funky? something else?

8 CONVERSATION *Which one is she?*

A ▶ Listen and practice.

Liz: Hi, Raoul! Good to see you!
   Where's Maggie?
Raoul: Oh, she couldn't make it.
   She went to a concert
   with Alex.
Liz: Oh! Well, why don't you go
   and talk to Julia? She doesn't
   know anyone here.
Raoul: Julia? Which one is she?
   Is she the woman wearing
   glasses over there?
Liz: No, she's the tall one in jeans.
   She's standing near the window.
Raoul: Oh, I'd like to meet her.

B ▶ Listen to the rest of the
conversation. Label Joe, Michiko,
Rosa, and John in the picture.

9 GRAMMAR FOCUS

Modifiers with participles and prepositions ⊙

Who's Raoul?	He's **the man**	**Participles**
Which one is Raoul?	He's **the one**	**wearing** a green shirt.
		talking to Liz.
		Prepositions
Who's Liz?	She's **the woman**	**with** short black hair.
Which one is Julia?	She's **the tall one**	**in** jeans.
Who are the Smiths?	They're **the people**	**next to** the window.
Which ones are the Smiths?	They're **the ones**	**on** the couch.

A Rewrite these statements using modifiers with participles or prepositions.

1. Clark is the tall guy. He's wearing a button-down shirt and cargo pants.
   Clark is the tall guy wearing a button-down shirt and cargo pants.

2. Adam and Louise are the good-looking couple. They're talking to Tom.
   ....

3. Lynne is the young girl. She's in a striped T-shirt and blue jeans.
   ....

4. Jessica is the attractive woman. She's sitting to the left of Antonio.
   ....

5. A.J. is the serious-looking boy. He's playing a video game.
   ....

B **PAIR WORK** Complete these questions using your classmates' names and information. Then take turns asking and answering the questions.

1. Who's the man sitting next to .... ?
2. Who's the woman wearing .... ?
3. Who is .... ?
4. Which one is .... ?
5. Who are the people .... ?
6. Who are the ones .... ?

10 PRONUNCIATION *Contrastive stress in responses*

A ⊙ Listen and practice. Notice how the stress changes to emphasize a contrast.

A: Is Anthony the one wearing the red shirt?

B: No, he's the one wearing the black shirt.

A: Is Judy the woman on the couch?

B: No, Diana is the woman on the couch.

B ⊙ Mark the stress changes in these conversations. Listen and check. Then practice the conversations.

A: Is Britney the one sitting next to Katy?

B: No, she's the one standing next to Katy.

A: Is Donald the one on the couch?

B: No, he's the one behind the couch.

DEAR KEN AND PIXIE

Your style questions answered!

Look at the pictures. What is each an example of? Match the descriptions with the pictures. a. mixing old and new   b. mixing baggy and slim   c. mixing colors and patterns

All of your questions this week are about mixing and matching styles, patterns, and colors.

Dear Ken and Pixie,
I'm reading a lot about how to mix prints in the latest fashion magazines. But when I wear different prints together, I look silly. What's the trick?
– Mixed-up

Dear Mixed-up,
It's not difficult to wear different prints together. Find the similarity in each item of clothing you want to wear. Mix two or three items with the same background color, like white or another neutral color. Mix a large print with a small one. Mix similar patterns, like stripes with plaid. But if you don't feel comfortable in it, don't wear it!

Dear Ken and Pixie,
In college, I wore vintage clothes, but now I'm 30 and need a modern look. How can I wear vintage styles without looking outdated?
– Oldie but Goodie

Dear Oldie but Goodie,
Vintage clothing is always in! But mix it with something new for a modern look. Wear a vintage shirt with pants. Pair an old belt with a new bag. Wear vintage shoes with new jeans. But sometimes you need to alter the clothes. For example, take a baggy vintage skirt and make it slim, or cut the shoulder pads out of a vintage jacket.

Dear Ken and Pixie,
I'm seeing both baggy pants and skinny pants on the designer runways. Also, short pants and long pants. What's in style?
– Confused Carrie

Dear Confused Carrie,
It's all in style! For pants, anything goes this year. The trick is to wear something on top that is the opposite of the style of the pants. So, if you're wearing baggy pants, try a slim shirt. If slim pants are your thing, wear a baggy sweater. Short pants? Try funky shoes. Wear long pants with your shirt tucked in and a belt.

A Read the webpage. Find the words in *italics* in the text. Then match each word with its meaning.

....	1. *neutral*	a.	not in style
....	2. *vintage*	b.	change
....	3. *outdated*	c.	slim
....	4. *alter*	d.	from the past but still in style
....	5. *baggy*	e.	without strong color
....	6. *skinny*	f.	loose fitting

B **PAIR WORK** Answer these questions.

1. Do you mix and match patterns and colors? What does your favorite outfit look like?
2. Do you have any vintage clothing? What time period is it from?
3. Do you wear clothes because they are fashionable or because they look good on you, or both?

10 Have you ever ridden a camel?

1 SNAPSHOT

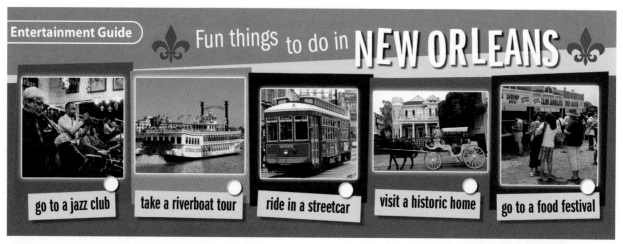

Entertainment Guide Fun things to do in **NEW ORLEANS**

go to a jazz club | take a riverboat tour | ride in a streetcar | visit a historic home | go to a food festival

Source: www.neworleansonline.com

Which activities have you done?
Check (✓) the activities you would like to try.

2 CONVERSATION A visit to New Orleans

A ▶ Listen and practice.

Jan: It's great to see you, Todd. Have you been in New Orleans long?

Todd: No, not really. Just a few days.

Jan: I can't wait to show you the city. Have you been to a jazz club yet?

Todd: Yeah, I've already been to one.

Jan: Oh. Well, how about a riverboat tour?

Todd: Uh, I've already done that, too.

Jan: Have you ridden in a streetcar? They're a lot of fun.

Todd: Actually, that's how I got here today.

Jan: Well, is there anything you want to do?

Todd: You know, I really just want to take it easy. My feet are killing me!

B ▶ Listen to the rest of the conversation. What do they plan to do tomorrow?

Present perfect; already, yet ▶

The present perfect is formed with the verb **have** + the past participle.		Contractions		
Have you **been** to a jazz club?		**I've**	=	I have
Yes, I**'ve been** to several.	No, I **haven't been** to one.	you**'ve**	=	you have
Has he **called** home lately?		he**'s**	=	he has
Yes, he**'s called** twice this week.	No, he **hasn't called** in months.	she**'s**	=	she has
Have they **eaten** dinner yet?		it**'s**	=	it has
Yes, they**'ve** already **eaten**.	No, they **haven't eaten** yet.	we**'ve**	=	we have
		they**'ve**	=	they have
		has**n't**	=	has not
		have**n't**	=	have not

A How many times have you done these things in the past week? Write your answers. Then compare with a partner.

1. clean the house
2. make your bed
3. cook dinner
4. do laundry
5. wash the dishes
6. go grocery shopping

regular past participles	
call	→ call**ed**
hike	→ hike**d**
jog	→ jog**ged**
try	→ tr**ied**

> I've cleaned the house once this week.
>
> OR
>
> I haven't cleaned the house this week.

irregular past participles	
be	→ **been**
do	→ **done**
eat	→ **eaten**
go	→ **gone**
have	→ **had**
make	→ **made**
ride	→ **ridden**
see	→ **seen**

B Complete these conversations using the present perfect. Then practice with a partner.

1. A: ....*Have*.... you ....*done*.... much exercise this week? (do)
   B: Yes, I .... already .... to aerobics class four times. (be)

2. A: .... you .... any sports this month? (play)
   B: No, I .... the time. (have)

3. A: How many movies .... you .... to this month? (be)
   B: Actually, I .... any yet. (see)

4. A: .... you .... to any interesting parties recently? (be)
   B: No, I .... to any parties for quite a while. (go)

5. A: .... you .... any friends today? (call)
   B: Yes, I .... already .... three calls. (make)

6. A: How many times .... you .... out to eat this week? (go)
   B: I .... at fast-food restaurants a couple of times. (eat)

C **PAIR WORK** Take turns asking the questions in part B. Give your own information when answering.

4 CONVERSATION *Actually, I have.*

A ▶ Listen and practice.

Peter: I'm sorry I'm late. Have you been here long?
Mandy: No, only for a few minutes.
Peter: Have you chosen a restaurant yet?
Mandy: I can't decide. Have you ever eaten Moroccan food?
Peter: No, I haven't. Is it good?
Mandy: It's delicious. I've had it several times.
Peter: Or how about Thai food? Have you ever had green curry?
Mandy: Actually, I have. I lived in Thailand as a teenager. I ate it a lot there.
Peter: I didn't know that. How long did you live there?
Mandy: I lived there for two years.

B ▶ Listen to the rest of the conversation.
Where do they decide to have dinner?

5 GRAMMAR FOCUS

> ### Present perfect vs. simple past ▶
>
> **Use the present perfect for an indefinite time in the past.**
> **Use the simple past for a specific event in the past.**
>
> | | |
> |---|---|
> | **Have** you ever **eaten** Moroccan food? | Yes, I **have**. I **ate** it once in Paris. |
> | | No, I **haven't**. I**'ve** never **eaten** it. |
> | **Have** you ever **had** green curry? | Yes, I **have**. I **tried** it several years ago. |
> | | No, I **haven't**. I**'ve** never **had** it. |

A Complete these conversations. Use the present perfect and simple past of the verbs given and short answers. Then practice with a partner.

1. A: .... you ever .... in a karaoke bar? (sing)
   B: Yes, I .... I .... in one on my birthday.

2. A: .... you ever .... something valuable? (lose)
   B: No, I .... But my brother .... his camera on a trip once.

3. A: .... you ever .... a traffic ticket? (get)
   B: Yes, I .... Once I .... a ticket and had to pay $50.

4. A: .... you ever .... a live concert? (see)
   B: Yes, I .... I .... the Black Eyed Peas at the stadium last year.

5. A: .... you ever .... late for an important appointment? (be)
   B: No, I .... But my sister .... 30 minutes late for her wedding!

B **PAIR WORK** Take turns asking the questions in part A.
Give your own information when answering.

For *and* since ▶

How long **did** you **live** in Thailand?	I **lived** there **for** two years. It was wonderful.
How long **have** you **lived** in Miami?	I**'ve lived** here **for** six months. I love it here.
	I**'ve lived** here **since** last year. I'm really happy here.

C Complete these sentences with *for* or *since*.
Then compare with a partner.

1. Pam was in Central America .... a month last year.
2. I've been a college student .... almost four years.
3. Hiroshi has been at work .... 6:00 A.M.
4. I haven't gone to a party .... a long time.
5. Josh lived in Venezuela .... two years as a kid.
6. My parents have been on vacation .... Monday.
7. Natalie was engaged to Danny .... six months.
8. Pat and Valeria have been best friends .... high school.

D **PAIR WORK** Ask and answer these questions.

How long have you had your current hairstyle?　　How long have you known your best friend?
How long have you studied at this school?　　How long have you been awake today?

> **expressions with *for***
>
> two weeks
> a few months
> several years
> a long time

> **expressions with *since***
>
> 6:45
> last weekend
> 1997
> elementary school

6 PRONUNCIATION Linked sounds

A ▶ Listen and practice. Notice how final /t/ and /d/ sounds in
verbs are linked to the vowels that follow them.

A: Have you cooked lunch yet?　　A: Have you ever tried Cuban food?

　　　　　　/t/　　　　　　　　　　　　　/d/
B: Yes, I've already cooked‿it.　　B: Yes, I tried‿it once in Miami.

B **PAIR WORK** Ask and answer these questions. Use *it* in your
responses. Pay attention to the linked sounds.

Have you ever cut your hair?
Have you ever tasted blue cheese?
Have you ever tried Korean food?
Have you ever lost your ID?
Have you looked at Unit 11 yet?

7 LISTENING I'm impressed!

▶ Listen to Clarice and Karl talk about interesting things they've
done recently. Complete the chart.

	Where they went	Why they liked it
Clarice	....	....
Karl	....	....

Have you ever ridden a camel? ▪ **67**

8 WORD POWER Activities

A Find two phrases to go with each verb. Write them in the chart.

a camel	a costume	iced coffee	a motorcycle	your phone	a truck
chicken's feet	herbal tea	your keys	octopus	a sports car	a uniform

eat	....	....	....
drink	....	....	....
drive	....	....	....
lose	....	....	....
ride	....	....	....
wear	....	....	....

B Add another phrase for each verb in part A.

9 SPEAKING Have you ever . . . ?

A **GROUP WORK** Ask your classmates questions about the activities in Exercise 8 or your own ideas.

A: Have you ever ridden a camel?
B: Yes, I have.
C: Really? Where were you?

B **CLASS ACTIVITY** Tell the class one interesting thing you learned about a classmate.

10 WRITING An email to an old friend

A Write an email to someone you haven't seen for a long time. Include three things you've done since you last saw that person.

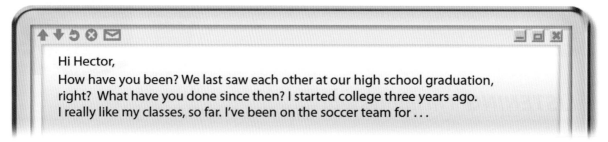

Hi Hector,
How have you been? We last saw each other at our high school graduation, right? What have you done since then? I started college three years ago. I really like my classes, so far. I've been on the soccer team for . . .

B **PAIR WORK** Exchange emails with a partner. Write a response to it.

11 INTERCHANGE 10 Lifestyle survey

What kind of lifestyle do you have? Go to Interchange 10 on page 125.

TAKING THE RISK
////////////////

Look at the pictures and skim the interviews. Then write the name of the sport below each picture.

Sports World magazine recently spoke with Josh Parker, Lisa Kim, and Alex Costas about risky sports.

SW: Wingsuit flying is a dangerous sport, Josh. What do you enjoy about it? And have you ever had an accident?

Josh: No, I've never been hurt. But, yes, it is dangerous, even for experienced flyers. I've been doing it for five years, but I still get a little nervous before I jump out of the plane. That's the most dangerous thing. Once, I jumped too fast, and I started to spin. That was scary! But it's amazing to be able to fly like a bird.

SW: Lisa, you've been kiteboarding for years now. What are some of the dangers?

Lisa: Oh, there are many dangers. When you're in the ocean, the conditions can be unpredictable. The wind can lift you up too fast and then drop you against something hard, like sand, or even water. You can also hit another surfer. But I like the challenge, and I like overcoming danger. That's why I do it.

SW: Alex, have you ever experienced any dangers while ice climbing?

Alex: Yes, absolutely. When you're high up on a mountain, the conditions are hard on the body. The air is thin, and it's very cold. I've seen some really dangerous storms. But the great thing about it is how you feel when you're done. Your body feels good, and you have a beautiful view of the snowy mountaintops.

▶ _____

▶ _____

////////////////

▶ _____

A Read the interviews. Then complete the chart.

	Sport	What they enjoy	The danger(s)
1. Josh	....	....	....
2. Lisa	....	....	....
3. Alex	....	....	....

B **PAIR WORK** Would you like to try any of these sports? Why or why not?

Units 9–10 Progress check

SELF-ASSESSMENT

How well can you do these things? Check (✓) the boxes.

I can	Very well	OK	A little
Ask about and describe people's appearance (Ex. 1)	☐	☐	☐
Identify people by describing what they're doing, what they're wearing, and where they are (Ex. 2)	☐	☐	☐
Find out whether or not things have been done (Ex. 3)	☐	☐	☐
Understand descriptions of experiences (Ex. 4)	☐	☐	☐
Ask and answer questions about experiences (Ex. 4)	☐	☐	☐
Find out how long people have done things (Ex. 5)	☐	☐	☐

 1 ROLE PLAY *Missing person*

Student A: One of your classmates is lost. You are talking to a police officer. Answer the officer's questions and describe your classmate.

Student B: You are a police officer. Someone is describing a lost classmate. Ask questions to complete the form. Can you identify the classmate?

Change roles and try the role play again.

MISSING PERSON REPORT

NAME _____   # 78439122475

HEIGHT: _____   WEIGHT: _____   AGE: _____

EYE COLOR		HAIR COLOR	
☐ BLUE	☐ BROWN	☐ BLOND	☐ BROWN
☐ GREEN	☐ HAZEL	☐ RED	☐ BLACK
		☐ GRAY	☐ BALD

CLOTHING: _____
_____

GLASSES, ETC: _____

2 SPEAKING Which one is . . . ?

A Look at this picture. How many sentences can you write to identify the people?

> Amy and T.J. are the people in sunglasses. They're the ones looking at the picture.

B PAIR WORK Close your books. Who do you remember? Take turns asking about the people.

A: Which one is Bill?
B: I think Bill is the guy sitting . . .

Kate

Louisa

Bill

Amy and T.J.

SPEAKING *Reminders*

A Imagine you are preparing for these situations. Make a list of four things you need to do for each situation.

Your first day of school is in a week.
You are moving to a new apartment.
You are going to the beach.

> "To do" list: first day of school
> 1. buy notebooks

B **PAIR WORK** Exchange lists. Take turns asking about what has been done. When answering, decide what you have or haven't done.

A: Have you bought notebooks yet?
B: Yes, I've already gotten them.

4 LISTENING *What have you done?*

A 🔘 Jamie is on a cruise. Listen to her talk about things she has done. Check (✓) the correct things.

- ☐ won a contest
- ☐ flown in a plane
- ☐ stayed in an expensive hotel
- ☐ met a famous person
- ☐ gone windsurfing
- ☐ lost her wallet
- ☐ been seasick
- ☐ kept a diary

B **GROUP WORK** Have you ever done the things in part A? Take turns asking about each thing.

5 SURVEY *How long . . . ?*

A Write answers to these questions using *for* and *since*.

How long have you . . . ?	My answers	Classmate's name
owned this book	....	....
studied English	....	....
known your best friend	....	....
lived in this town or city	....	....
been a student	....	....

B **CLASS ACTIVITY** Go around the class. Find someone who has the same answers. Write a classmate's names only once.

WHAT'S NEXT?

Look at your Self-assessment again. Do you need to review anything?

11 It's a very exciting place!

1 WORD POWER Adjectives

A **PAIR WORK** Match each word in column A with its opposite in column B. Then add two more pairs of adjectives to the list.

beautiful

A	B
1. beautiful	a. boring
2. cheap	b. crowded
3. clean	c. dangerous
4. interesting	d. expensive
5. quiet	e. noisy
6. relaxing	f. polluted
7. safe	g. stressful
8. spacious	h. ugly
9.	i. ....
10.	j. ....

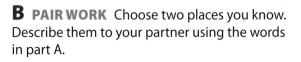

ugly

B **PAIR WORK** Choose two places you know. Describe them to your partner using the words in part A.

2 CONVERSATION It's a fairly big city.

A  Listen and practice.

Eric: So, where are you from, Carmen?
Carmen: I'm from San Juan, Puerto Rico.
Eric: Wow, I've heard that's a really nice city.
Carmen: Yeah, it is. The weather is great, and there are some fantastic beaches nearby.
Eric: Is it expensive there?
Carmen: No, it's not very expensive. Prices are pretty reasonable.
Eric: How big is the city?
Carmen: It's a fairly big city. It's not *too* big, though.
Eric: It sounds perfect to me. Maybe I should plan a trip there sometime.

B Listen to the rest of the conversation. What does Carmen say about entertainment in San Juan?

San Juan

Adverbs before adjectives ▶

San Juan is **really** nice.   It's a **really** nice city.
It's **fairly** big.   It's a **fairly** big city.
It's not **very** expensive.   It's not a **very** expensive place.

It's **too** noisy, and it's **too** crowded for me.

adverbs
extremely
very
really
pretty
fairly
somewhat
too

A Match the questions with the answers. Then practice the conversations with a partner.

1. What's Seoul like?
   Is it an interesting place? ....

2. Do you like your hometown?
   Why or why not? ....

3. What's Sydney like?
   I've never been there. ....

4. Have you ever been to
   São Paulo? ....

5. What's the weather like
   in Chicago? ....

a. Oh, really? It's beautiful and very clean. It has a great harbor and beautiful beaches.

b. Yes, I have. It's an extremely large and crowded place, but I love it. It has excellent restaurants.

c. It's really nice in the summer, but it's too cold for me in the winter.

d. Not really. It's too small, and it's really boring. That's why I moved away.

e. Yes. It has amazing shopping, and the people are pretty friendly.

Conjunctions ▶

It's a big city, **and** the weather is nice.   It's a big city. It's not too big, **though**.
It's a big city, **but** it's not too big.   It's a big city. It's not too big, **however**.

B Choose the correct conjunctions and rewrite the sentences.

1. Taipei is very nice. Everyone is extremely friendly. (and / but)

   ....

2. The streets are crowded. It's easy to get around. (and / though)

   ....

3. The weather is nice. Summers get pretty hot. (and / however)

   ....

4. Shopping is great. You have to bargain in the markets. (and / but)

   ....

5. It's an amazing city. I love to go there. (and / however)

   ....

C **GROUP WORK** Describe three cities or towns in your country. State two positive features and one negative feature for each.

A: Lima is very exciting and there are a lot of things to do, but it's too cold.
B: The weather in Shanghai is …

4 LISTENING My hometown

▶ Listen to Joyce and Nicholas talk about their hometowns.
What do they say? Check (✓) the correct boxes.

	Big?		Interesting?		Expensive?		Beautiful?	
	Yes	No	Yes	No	Yes	No	Yes	No
1. Joyce	☐	☐	☐	☐	☐	☐	☐	☐
2. Nicholas	☐	☐	☐	☐	☐	☐	☐	☐

5 WRITING An interesting place

A Write about an interesting town or city for tourists to visit in your country.

> Otavalo is a very interesting town in Ecuador. It's to the north of Quito. It has a fantastic market, and a lot of tourists go there to buy local handicrafts. The scenery around Otavalo is very pretty and . . .

B PAIR WORK Exchange papers and read each other's articles.
Which place sounds more interesting?

6 SNAPSHOT

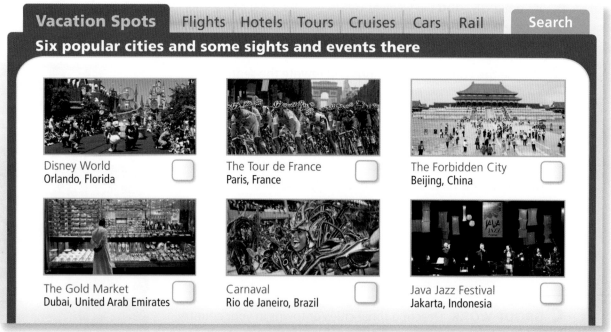

| Vacation Spots | Flights | Hotels | Tours | Cruises | Cars | Rail | Search |

Six popular cities and some sights and events there

Disney World
Orlando, Florida ☐

The Tour de France
Paris, France ☐

The Forbidden City
Beijing, China ☐

The Gold Market
Dubai, United Arab Emirates ☐

Carnaval
Rio de Janeiro, Brazil ☐

Java Jazz Festival
Jakarta, Indonesia ☐

Source: www.fodors.com

Which places would you like to visit? Why?
Put the places you would like to visit in order from most interesting to least interesting.
What three other places in the world would you like to visit? Why?

7 **CONVERSATION** *What should I see there?*

A  Listen and practice.

Thomas: Can you tell me a little about Mexico City?
Elena: Sure. What would you like to know?
Thomas: Well, I'm going to be there next month, but for only two days. What should I see?
Elena: Oh, you should definitely visit the Palace of Fine Arts. It's really beautiful.
Thomas: OK. Anything else?
Elena: You shouldn't miss the Museum of Modern Art. It has some amazing paintings.
Thomas: Great! And is there anything I can do for free?
Elena: Sure. You can walk in the parks, go to outdoor markets, or just watch people. It's a fascinating city!

B Listen to the rest of the conversation.
Where is Thomas from? What should you do there?

8 *GRAMMAR FOCUS*

> **Modal verbs can and should**
>
> What **can** I do in Mexico City?   What **should** I see there?
> You **can** go to outdoor markets.   You **should** visit the Palace of Fine Arts.
> You **can't** visit some museums on Mondays.   You **shouldn't** miss the Museum of Modern Art.

A Complete these conversations using *can, can't, should,* or *shouldn't*.
Then practice with a partner.

1. A: I .... decide where to go on my vacation.
   B: You .... go to India. It's my favorite place to visit.
2. A: I'm planning to go to Bogotá next year. When do you think I .... go?
   B: You .... go anytime. The weather is nice almost all year.
3. A: .... I rent a car when I arrive in Cairo? What do you recommend?
   B: No, you .... definitely use the subway. It's fast and efficient.
4. A: Where .... I get some nice jewelry in Bangkok?
   B: You .... miss the weekend market. It's the best place for bargains.
5. A: What .... I see from the Eiffel Tower?
   B: You .... see all of Paris, but in bad weather, you .... see anything.

B Write answers to these questions about your country.
Then compare with a partner.

What time of year should you go there?   What can you do for free?
What are three things you can do there?   What shouldn't a visitor miss?

9 PRONUNCIATION Can't *and* shouldn't

A ▶ Listen and practice these statements. Notice how the *t* in **can't** and **shouldn't** is not strongly pronounced.

You can get a taxi easily.
You can**'t** get a taxi easily.
You should visit in the summer.
You shouldn**'t** visit in the summer.

B ▶ Listen to four sentences. Circle the modal verb you hear.

1. can / can't   2. should / shouldn't   3. can / can't   4. should / shouldn't

10 LISTENING Three capital cities

A ▶ Listen to speakers talk about Japan, Argentina, and Egypt. Complete the chart.

	Capital city	What visitors should see or do
1. Japan	....	....
2. Argentina	....	....
3. Egypt	....	....

B ▶ Listen again. One thing about each country is incorrect. What is it?

11 SPEAKING Interesting places

GROUP WORK Has anyone visited an interesting place in your country? Find out more about it. Start like this and ask questions like the ones below.

A: I visited Istanbul once.
B: Really? What's the best time of year to visit?
A: It's nice all year. I went in March.
C: What's the weather like then?

What's the best time of year to visit?
What's the weather like then?
What should tourists see and do there?
What special foods can you eat?
What's the shopping like?
What things should people buy?
What else can visitors do there?

Istanbul, Turkey

12 INTERCHANGE 11 City guide

Make a guide to fun places in your city. Go to Interchange 11 on page 126.

Scan the email messages. What city has a puppet show? What city has two personalities? What city is famous for leather?

Fez is so interesting! I've been to the medina (the old city) every day. It has walls all the way around it, and more than 9,000 streets! It's always crowded and noisy. My favorite places to visit are the small shops where people make local crafts. Fez is famous for its leather products. I visited a place where they dye the leather in dozens of beautiful colors.

I came at the perfect time, because the World Sacred Music festival is happening right now!

Kathy

I've discovered that Cartagena has two different personalities. One is a lively city with fancy restaurants and crowded old plazas. And the other is a quiet and relaxing place with sandy beaches.

If you come here, you should stay in the historic district – a walled area with great shopping, nightclubs, and restaurants. It has some wonderful old Spanish buildings.

Last night, I learned some salsa steps at a great dance club.

Today, I went on a canoe tour of La Ciénaga mangrove forest.

Mike

Hanoi is the capital of Vietnam and its second-largest city. It's a fun city, but six days is not enough time for a visit. I'm staying near the Old Quarter of the city. It's a great place to meet people. Last night I went to a water puppet show. Tomorrow I'm going to Ha Long Bay.

I took a cooking class at the Vietnam Culinary School. I bought some fruits and vegetables at a local market and then prepared some local dishes. My food was really delicious! I'll cook you something when I get home.

Belinda

A Read the emails. Check (✓) the cities where you can do these things. Then complete the chart with examples from the emails.

Activity	Fez	Cartagena	Hanoi	Specific examples
1. go shopping	☐	☐	☐	....
2. see old buildings	☐	☐	☐	....
3. go dancing	☐	☐	☐	....
4. attend a festival	☐	☐	☐	....
5. take a boat trip	☐	☐	☐	....

B **PAIR WORK** Which city is the most interesting to you? Why?

12 It really works!

Common Health Complaints

- a headache
- a backache
- sore muscles
- a stomachache
- a cold
- a cough
- the flu
- insomnia

Source: National Center for Health Statistics

Check (✓) the health problems you have had recently.
What do you do for the health problems you checked?
How many times have you been sick in the past year?

2 CONVERSATION *Health problems*

A ▶ Listen and practice.

Joan: Hi, Craig! How are you?
Craig: Not so good. I have a terrible cold.
Joan: Really? That's too bad! You should be at home in bed. It's really important to get a lot of rest.
Craig: Yeah, you're right.
Joan: And have you taken anything for it?
Craig: No, I haven't.
Joan: Well, it's sometimes helpful to eat garlic soup. Just chop up a whole head of garlic and cook it in chicken stock. Try it! It really works!
Craig: Yuck! That sounds awful!

B ▶ Listen to advice from two more of Craig's co-workers. What do they suggest?

78

Adjective + infinitive; noun + infinitive ▸

What should you do for a cold?	It's **important**	**to get** a lot of rest.
	It's sometimes **helpful**	**to eat** garlic soup.
	It's a **good idea**	**to take** some vitamin C.

A Look at these health problems. Choose several pieces of good advice for each problem.

Problems

1. a sore throat ....
2. a cough ....
3. a backache ....
4. a fever ....
5. a toothache ....
6. a bad headache ....
7. a burn ....
8. the flu ....

Advice

a. take some vitamin C
b. put some ointment on it
c. drink lots of liquids
d. go to bed and rest
e. put a heating pad on it
f. put it under cold water
g. take some aspirin
h. see a dentist
i. see a doctor
j. get some medicine

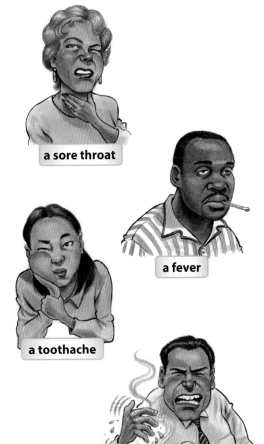

a sore throat

a fever

a toothache

a burn

B **GROUP WORK** Talk about the problems in part A and give advice. What other advice do you have?

A: What should you do for a sore throat?
B: It's a good idea to get some medicine from the drugstore.
C: And it's important to drink lots of liquids and . . .

C Write advice for these problems. (You will use this advice in Exercise 4.)

a cold   sore eyes   a sunburn   sore muscles

> For a cold, it's a good idea to . . .

A Listen and practice. In conversation, **to** is often reduced to /tə/.

A: What should you do for a fever?
B: It's important **to** take some aspirin. And it's a good idea **to** see a doctor.

B **PAIR WORK** Look back at Exercise 3, part C. Ask for and give advice about each health problem. Pay attention to the pronunciation of **to**.

5 INTERCHANGE 12 *Help!*

Play a board game. Go to Interchange 12 on page 127.

6 DISCUSSION *Difficult situations*

A GROUP WORK Imagine these situations are true for you. Get three suggestions for each one.

I get really hungry before I go to bed.
I sometimes feel really stressed.
I need to study, but I can't concentrate.
I feel sick before every exam.
I forget about half the new words I learn.
I get nervous when I speak English to foreigners.

A: I get really hungry before I go to bed. What should I do?
B: It's a bad idea to eat late at night.
C: It's sometimes helpful to drink herbal tea.

B CLASS ACTIVITY Have any of the above situations happened to you recently? Share what you did with the class.

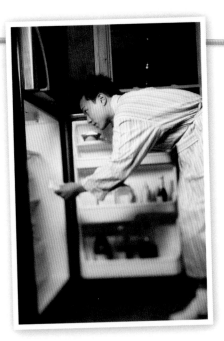

7 WORD POWER *Containers*

A Use the words in the list to complete these expressions. Then compare with a partner.

bag   jar
bottle   pack
box   stick
can   tube

1. a .... of toothpaste
2. a .... of aspirin
3. a .... of bandages
4. a .... of shaving cream
5. a .... of tissues
6. a .... of face cream
7. a .... of cough drops
8. a .... of deodorant

B PAIR WORK What is one more thing you can buy in each of the containers above?

"You can buy a bag of breath mints."

C PAIR WORK What are the five most useful items in your medicine cabinet?

8 CONVERSATION *What do you suggest?*

A ▶ Listen and practice.

Pharmacist: Hi. May I help you?

Mrs. Webb: Yes, please. Could I have something for a cough? I think I'm getting a cold.

Pharmacist: Sure. Why don't you try these cough drops? They work very well.

Mrs. Webb: OK, I'll take one box. And what do you suggest for dry skin?

Pharmacist: Well, you could get a jar of this new lotion. It's very good.

Mrs. Webb: OK. And one more thing. My husband has no energy these days. Can you suggest anything?

Pharmacist: He should try some of these multivitamins. They're excellent.

Mrs. Webb: Great! May I have three large bottles, please?

B ▶ Listen to the pharmacist talk to the next customer. What does the customer want?

9 GRAMMAR FOCUS

> **Modal verbs can, could, may *for requests; suggestions*** ▶
>
> | | |
> |---|---|
> | **Can/May** I help you? | What do you suggest/have for dry skin? |
> | **Can** I have a box of cough drops? | You could try this lotion. |
> | **Could** I have something for a cough? | You should get some skin cream. |
> | **May** I have a bottle of aspirin? | Why don't you try this new ointment? |

Circle the correct words. Then compare and practice with a partner.

1. A: **Can / Could** I help you?
   B: Yes. **May / Do** I have something for itchy eyes?
   A: Sure. You **could / may** try a bottle of eyedrops.

2. A: What do you **suggest / try** for sore muscles?
   B: Why don't you **suggest / try** this ointment? It's excellent.
   A: OK. I'll take it.

3. A: Could I **suggest / have** a box of bandages, please?
   B: Here you are.
   A: And what do you **suggest / try** for insomnia?
   B: You **should / may** try this herbal tea. It's very relaxing.
   A: OK. Thanks.

10 *LISTENING* *Try this!*

A ▶ Listen to four people talk to a pharmacist. Check (✓) each person's problem.

1. ☐ The man's feet are sore.
   ☐ The man's feet are itchy.
2. ☐ The woman can't eat.
   ☐ The woman has an upset stomach.

3. ☐ The man has difficulty sleeping.
   ☐ The man is sleeping too much.
4. ☐ The woman burned her hand.
   ☐ The woman has a bad sunburn.

B ▶ Listen again. What does the pharmacist suggest for each person?

11 *ROLE PLAY* *Can I help you?*

Student A: You are a customer in a drugstore. You need:

something for low energy
something for the flu
something for a backache
something for dry skin
something for an upset stomach
something for sore feet

Ask for some suggestions.

Student B: You are a pharmacist in a drugstore. A customer needs some things. Make some suggestions.

Change roles and try the role play again.

12 *WRITING* *A letter to an advice columnist*

A Read these letters to an online advice columnist.

Dear Fix-it Fred

Dear Fix-it Fred

I have a problem and need your advice. My parents don't like how I dress. I think I have an interesting style, but my parents say I just look strange. Weren't they ever teenagers? Can you please help?

Funky Frida

Dear Fix-it Fred

Several months ago, I started college. I study a lot and have a part-time job, so I don't have much of a social life. I haven't made many friends, but I really want to. What do you suggest?

Too Busy

B Now imagine you want some advice about a problem. Write a short letter to an advice columnist. Think of an interesting way to sign it.

C GROUP WORK Exchange letters. Read and write down some advice at the bottom of each letter. Then share the most interesting letter and advice with the class.

WORLD NEWS

HOME | LOG IN | SETTINGS

HOME | CURRENT ISSUE | ARCHIVES | WEB EXTRAS | RADIO | CONTACT US | SUBSCRIBE

Rain Forest Remedies?

Look at the title, pictures, and captions. What do you think the article is about?

Carol writes a column on health.
Recently she took a trip to Tortuguero National Park in Costa Rica.

1 Rodrigo Bonilla turns off the motor of the boat. We get off the boat and follow him along the path into the rain forest. Above us, a monkey with a baby hangs from a tree.

2 On this hot January day, Rodrigo is not looking for wild animals, but for medicinal plants – plants that can cure or treat illnesses. Medicinal plants grow in rain forests around the world.

A broom tree

3 Rodrigo is Costa Rican. He learned about jungle medicine from his grandmother. He shows us many different plants, such as the broom tree. He tells us that parts of the broom tree can help stop bleeding.

4 People have always used natural products as medicine. In fact, about 50 percent of Western medicines, such as aspirin, come from natural sources. And some animals eat certain kinds of plants when they are sick.

5 This is why medical researchers are so interested in plants. Many companies are now working with local governments and searching the rain forests for medicinal plants.

6 So far, the search has not produced any new medicines. But it's a good idea to keep looking. That's why we are now here in the Costa Rican rain forest.

MORE >>

A Read the article. Then check (✓) the best description of the article.

☐ 1. The article starts with a description and then gives facts.
☐ 2. The article gives the writer's opinion.
☐ 3. The article starts with facts and then gives advice.

B Answer these questions. Then write the number of the paragraph where you find each answer.

.... Where did Rodrigo learn about jungle medicine?
.... Who is interested in studying medicinal plants?
.... What is Rodrigo looking for in the rain forest?
.... How many new medicines have come from Rodrigo's search?
.... How many Western medicines come from natural sources?

C **GROUP WORK** Can you think of other reasons why rain forests are important?

Units 11–12 Progress check

SELF-ASSESSMENT

How well can you do these things? Check (✓) the boxes.

I can	Very well	OK	A little
Understand descriptions of towns and cities (Ex. 1)	☐	☐	☐
Get useful information about towns and cities (Ex. 1, 2)	☐	☐	☐
Describe towns and cities (Ex. 2)	☐	☐	☐
Ask for and make suggestions on practical questions (Ex. 2, 3, 4)	☐	☐	☐
Ask for and give advice about problems (Ex. 3, 4)	☐	☐	☐

1 LISTENING *I'm from Honolulu.*

A ▶ Listen to Jenny talk about Honolulu. What does she say about these things? Complete the chart.

1. size of city ....
2. weather ....
3. prices of things ....
4. most famous place ....

B Write sentences comparing Honolulu with your hometown. Then discuss with a partner.

> Honolulu isn't too big, but Seoul is really big.

2 ROLE PLAY *My hometown*

Student A: Imagine you are planning to visit Student B's hometown. Ask questions using the ones in the box or your own questions.

Student B: Answer Student A's questions about your hometown.

A: What's your hometown like?
B: It's quiet but fairly interesting. . . .

possible questions

What's your hometown like?
How big is it?
What's the weather like?
Is it expensive?
What should you see there?
What can you do there?

Change roles and try the role play again.

3 DISCUSSION *Medicines and remedies*

A **GROUP WORK** Write advice and remedies for these problems. Then discuss your ideas in groups.

| a stomachache | an insect bite | a nosebleed | the hiccups |

> For a stomachache, it's a good idea to . . .

A: What can you do for a stomachache?
B: I think it's a good idea to buy a bottle of antacid.
C: Yes. And it's helpful to drink herbal tea.

B **GROUP WORK** What health problems do you visit a doctor for? go to a drugstore for? use a home remedy for? Ask for advice and remedies.

4 SPEAKING *Advice column*

A **GROUP WORK** Look at these problems from an advice column. Suggest advice for each problem. Then choose the best advice.

I'm visiting the United States. I'm staying with a family while I'm here. What small gifts can I get for them?

My co-worker always talks loudly to her friends – during work hours. I can't concentrate! What can I do?

Our school wants to buy some new gym equipment. Can you suggest some good ways to raise money?

A: Why doesn't she give them some flowers? They're always nice.
B: That's a good idea. Or she could bring chocolates.
C: I think she should . . .

B **CLASS ACTIVITY** Share your group's advice for each problem with the class.

WHAT'S NEXT?

Look at your Self-assessment again. Do you need to review anything?

13 May I take your order?

FOOD FIRSTS

NOODLES
first made in China around 1000 B.C.E.

COFFEE
first farmed in the Middle East in 850

CHOCOLATE
brought to Spain from Mexico in 1520

FRENCH FRIES
first made in Belgium around 1680

SUSHI
modern-style sushi first made in Japan in the 1700s

THE SANDWICH
named for the English Earl of Sandwich in 1760

PIZZA
first pizzeria in New York City opened in 1895

THE HAMBURGER
invented in Connecticut, USA, in 1900

Sources: *New York Public Library Book of Chronologies*; www.digitalsushi.net; www.belgianfries.com

What are these foods made of?
Put the foods in order from your favorite to your least favorite.
What are three other foods you enjoy?

2 CONVERSATION *Getting something to eat*

A ▶ Listen and practice.

Jeff: Say, do you want to get something to eat?
Bob: Sure. I'm tired of studying.
Jeff: So am I. So, what do you think of Indian food?
Bob: I love it, but I'm not really in the mood for it today.
Jeff: Yeah. I'm not either, I guess. It's a bit spicy.
Bob: Do you like Japanese food?
Jeff: Yeah, I like it a lot.
Bob: So do I. And I know a great restaurant near here – it's called Iroha.
Jeff: Oh, I've always wanted to go there.

B ▶ Listen to the rest of the conversation. What time do they decide to have dinner? Where do they decide to meet?

So, too, neither, either ▶

I like Japanese food a lot.
So do I./I do, **too**.
Really? I don't like it very much.

I'm crazy about Italian food.
So am I./I am, **too**.
Oh, I'm not.

I can eat really spicy food.
So can I./I can, **too**.
Really? I can't.

I don't like salty food.
Neither do I./I don't **either**.
Oh, I like it a lot.

I'm not in the mood for Indian food.
Neither am I./I'm not **either**.
Really? I am.

I can't stand fast food.
Neither can I./I can't **either**.
Oh, I love it!

healthy   salty   spicy   bland

greasy   rich   delicious

A Write responses to show agreement with these statements.
Then compare with a partner.

1. I'm not crazy about French food. ....
2. I can eat any kind of food. ....
3. I think Mexican food is delicious. ....
4. I can't stand greasy food. ....
5. I don't like salty food. ....
6. I'm in the mood for something spicy. ....
7. I'm tired of fast food. ....
8. I don't enjoy rich food very much. ....
9. I always eat healthy food. ....
10. I can't eat bland food. ....

B **PAIR WORK** Take turns responding to the statements in part A again.
Give your own opinion when responding.

C Write statements about these things. (You will use the statements in Exercise 4.)

1. two kinds of food you like
2. two kinds of food you can't stand
3. two kinds of food you are in the mood for

4 *PRONUNCIATION* *Stress in responses*

A ▶ Listen and practice. Notice how the last word of each response is stressed.

●	●	●	●
I do, too.	So do I.	I don't either.	Neither do I.
I am, too.	So am I.	I'm not either.	Neither am I.
I can, too.	So can I.	I can't either.	Neither can I.

B **PAIR WORK** Read and respond to the statements you wrote in Exercise 3, part C. Pay attention to the stress in your responses.

5 *WORD POWER* *Food categories*

A Complete the chart. Then add one more word to each category.

bread	fish	mangoes	peas	shrimp
chicken	grapes	octopus	potatoes	strawberries
corn	lamb	pasta	rice	turkey

Meat	Seafood	Fruit	Vegetables	Grains
....	....	....	....	....
....	....	....	....	....
....	....	....	....	....
....	....	....	....	....

B **GROUP WORK** What's your favorite food in each category? Are there any you haven't tried?

6 *CONVERSATION* *Ordering a meal*

A ▶ Listen and practice.

Server: May I take your order?
Customer: Yes. I'd like the spicy fish and rice.
Server: All right. And would you like a salad?
Customer: Yes, I'll have a mixed green salad.
Server: OK. What kind of dressing would you like?
We have blue cheese and vinaigrette.
Customer: Blue cheese, please.
Server: And would you like anything to drink?
Customer: Yes, I'd like a large iced tea, please.

B ▶ Listen to the server talk to the next customer.
What does she order?

TODAY'S SPECIALS
CHEESEBURGER AND FRIES
TURKEY SANDWICH WITH CHIPS
CHEESE PASTA AND SALAD

Modal verbs would and will for requests ▶

What **would** you **like**?	**I'd like** the fish and rice. **I'll have** a small salad.	*Contractions* **I'll** = I will
What kind of dressing **would** you **like**?	**I'd like** blue cheese, please. **I'll have** vinaigrette.	**I'd** = I would
What **would** you **like** to drink?	**I'd like** an iced tea. **I'll have** coffee.	
Would you **like** anything else?	Yes, please. **I'd like** some water. No, thank you. That**'ll be** all.	

Complete this conversation. Then practice with a partner.

Server: What .... you like to order?
Customer: I .... have the spicy chicken.
Server: .... you like rice or potatoes?
Customer: I .... like rice, please.
Server: OK. And .... you like anything to drink?
Customer: I .... just have a glass of water.
Server: Would you .... anything else?
Customer: No, that .... be all for now, thanks.

Later

Server: Would you .... dessert?
Customer: Yes, I .... like ice cream.
Server: What flavor .... you like?
Customer: Hmm. I .... have strawberry, please.

8 ROLE PLAY *In a coffee shop*

Student A: You are a customer in a coffee shop. Order what you want for lunch.
Student B: You are the server. Take your customer's order.

Today's Lunch Specials

Spicy beef and potatoes   Vegetable curry and rice
Lamb with french fries   Chicken salad sandwich
Shrimp pizza and salad   Sushi plate with miso soup
DRINKS
Coffee   Tea   Soda   Milk   Fresh juice
DESSERTS
Ice cream   Chocolate cake   Apple pie   Fresh fruit

Change roles and try the role play again.

9 LISTENING Let's order.

A ▶ Listen to Rex and Hannah order in a restaurant.
What did each of them order? Fill in their check.

Phil's DINER   No. 399825

....

....

....

....

....

....

Thank You!   **TOTAL** _____

B ▶ Listen to the rest of the conversation. Circle the two items that the server forgot to bring.

10 INTERCHANGE 13 Plan a menu

Create a menu of dishes to offer at your very own restaurant. Go to Interchange 13 on page 128.

11 WRITING A restaurant review

A Have you eaten out recently? Write a restaurant review.
Answer these questions and add ideas of your own.

What's the name of the restaurant?
When did you go there?
What did you have?
What did/didn't you like about it?
Would you recommend it? Why or why not?

| Overview | Review | Menu | Photos | | Search |

Luigi's ★★★★☆

Last week, I had lunch at Luigi's, a new Italian restaurant in my neighborhood.
I had a green salad and a cheese pizza. For dessert, I had chocolate cake.
The pizza was excellent, but the salad wasn't very good. The lettuce wasn't
very fresh. The cake was rich and delicious. I would recommend this restaurant
because the pizza is great and not very expensive.

B GROUP WORK Take turns reading your reviews.
Which restaurant would you like to try?

To Tip or Not to Tip?

Scan the article. How much should you tip someone in the United States who: carries your suitcase at a hotel? parks your car? serves you in a fast-food restaurant?

The word *tip* comes from an old English slang word that means "to give." It's both a noun and a verb. People in the U.S. usually tip people in places like restaurants, airports, hotels, and hair salons. People who work in these places often get paid low wages. A tip shows that the customer is pleased with the service.

Sometimes it's hard to know how much to tip. The size of the tip usually depends on the service. People such as parking valets or bellhops usually get smaller tips. The tip for people such as taxi drivers and servers is usually larger. Here are a few guidelines for tipping in the United States:

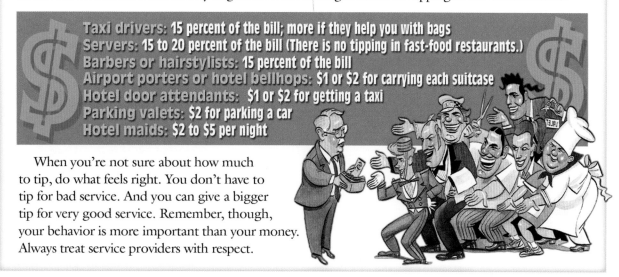

Taxi drivers: 15 percent of the bill; more if they help you with bags
Servers: 15 to 20 percent of the bill (There is no tipping in fast-food restaurants.)
Barbers or hairstylists: 15 percent of the bill
Airport porters or hotel bellhops: $1 or $2 for carrying each suitcase
Hotel door attendants: $1 or $2 for getting a taxi
Parking valets: $2 for parking a car
Hotel maids: $2 to $5 per night

When you're not sure about how much to tip, do what feels right. You don't have to tip for bad service. And you can give a bigger tip for very good service. Remember, though, your behavior is more important than your money. Always treat service providers with respect.

A Read the article. Find the words in italics in the article. Then check (✓) the meaning of each word.

1. *wages*
   - ☐ regular pay for a job
   - ☐ tips received for a job

2. *pleased*
   - ☐ happy or satisfied
   - ☐ annoyed or bothered

3. *depend on*
   - ☐ be the same as
   - ☐ change according to

4. *behavior*
   - ☐ a way of acting
   - ☐ a way of feeling

5. *treat*
   - ☐ ignore
   - ☐ act toward

6. *respect*
   - ☐ courtesy
   - ☐ rudeness

B Check (✓) the statements that describe appropriate tipping behavior. For the other items, what is acceptable?

- ☐ 1. Your haircut costs $40. You love it. You tip the stylist $3.
- ☐ 2. A porter at the airport helps you with three suitcases. You tip him $6.
- ☐ 3. Your fast-food meal costs $8. You don't leave a tip.
- ☐ 4. You stay in a hotel for a week. You leave a $10 tip for the hotel maid.
- ☐ 5. Your taxi ride costs $14. The driver carries your bag. You tip him $3.

C GROUP WORK Is tipping customary in your country? Do you like the idea of tipping? Why or why not?

14 The biggest and the best!

WORD POWER *Geography*

A Label the picture with words from the list. Then compare with a partner.

a. beach
b. desert
c. forest
d. hill
e. island
f. lake
g. mountain
h. ocean
i. river
j. valley
k. volcano
l. waterfall

B **PAIR WORK** What other geography words can you think of? Do you see any of them in the picture above?

C **GROUP WORK** Try to think of famous examples for each item in part A.

A: A famous beach is Waikiki in Hawaii.
B: And the Sahara is a famous . . .

2 CONVERSATION *Which is larger?*

A ▶ Listen and practice.

Mike: Here's an interesting geography quiz.
Wendy: Oh, I love geography. Ask me the questions.
Mike: Sure, first question. Which country is larger,
China or Canada?
Wendy: I know. Canada is larger than China.
Mike: OK, next. What's the longest river in the Americas?
Wendy: Hmm, I think it's the Mississippi.
Mike: Here's a hard one. Which country is more crowded,
Monaco or Singapore?
Wendy: I'm not sure. I think Monaco is more crowded.
Mike: OK, one more. Which South American capital city
is the highest: La Paz, Quito, or Bogotá?
Wendy: Oh, that's easy. Bogotá is the highest.

B ▶ Listen to the rest of the conversation. How many
questions did Wendy get right?

3 GRAMMAR FOCUS

Comparisons with adjectives ▶

Which country is **larger**, Canada or China?
  Canada is **larger than** China.

Which city has **the largest** population:
Tokyo, Mexico City, or São Paulo?
  Tokyo has **the largest** population of the three.

What is **the most beautiful** mountain in the world?
  I think Mount Fuji is **the most beautiful**.

Adjective	Comparative	Superlative
long	longer	the longest
dry	drier	the driest
big	bigger	the biggest
famous	more famous	the most famous
beautiful	more beautiful	the most beautiful
good	better	the best
bad	worse	the worst

A Complete questions 1 to 4 with comparatives and questions
5 to 8 with superlatives. Then ask and answer the questions.

1. Which country is .... , Monaco or Vatican City? (small)
2. Which waterfall is .... , Niagara Falls or Victoria Falls? (high)
3. Which city is .... , Hong Kong or Cairo? (crowded)
4. Which lake is .... , the Caspian Sea or Lake Superior? (large)
5. Which is .... : Mount Aconcagua, Mount Everest, or Mount Fuji? (high)
6. What is .... river in the world, the Mekong, the Nile, or the Amazon? (long)
7. Which city is .... : London, Tokyo, or Moscow? (expensive)
8. What is .... ocean in the world, the Pacific, the Atlantic, or the Arctic? (deep)

B **CLASS ACTIVITY** Write four questions like those in part A about your
country or other countries. Then ask your questions around the class.

4 PRONUNCIATION *Questions of choice*

A ▶ Listen and practice. Notice how the intonation in questions of choice drops, then rises, and then drops.

Which city is more crowded, Hong Kong or Cairo?

Which city is the most expensive: London, Tokyo, or Moscow?

B **PAIR WORK** Take turns asking these questions. Pay attention to your intonation. Can you guess the answers?

Which desert is bigger, the Gobi or the Sahara?
Which city is higher, Denver or New Orleans?
Which ocean is the smallest: the Arctic, the Indian, or the Atlantic?
Which mountains are the highest: the Alps, the Rockies, or the Himalayas?

5 SPEAKING *Our recommendations*

GROUP WORK Imagine these people are planning to visit your country. What would they enjoy doing? Agree on a recommendation for each person.

Molly
"I really like quiet places where I can relax, hike, and enjoy the views. I can't stand big crowds."

Rod
"I love to eat in nice restaurants, go dancing, and stay out late at night. I don't like small towns."

Teresa
"My favorite activity is shopping. I love to buy gifts to take home. I don't like modern shopping malls."

A: Molly should go to . . . because it has the best views in the country, and it's very quiet.
B: Or what about . . . ? I think the views there are more beautiful.
C: She also likes to hike, so . . .

6 LISTENING *Game show*

▶ Listen to three people on a TV game show. Check (✓) the correct answers.

1. ☐ the Statue of Liberty
   ☐ the Eiffel Tower
   ☐ the Panama Canal

2. ☐ Niagara Falls
   ☐ Angel Falls
   ☐ Victoria Falls

3. ☐ gold
   ☐ butter
   ☐ feathers

4. ☐ the U.S.
   ☐ China
   ☐ Canada

5. ☐ India
   ☐ Russia
   ☐ China

6. ☐ Australia
   ☐ Argentina
   ☐ Brazil

INTERCHANGE 14 *How much do you know?*

You probably know more than you think! Take a quiz.
Go to Interchange 14 on page 129.

8 SNAPSHOT

The World We Live In

■ **France is the most popular country to visit. It has about 78 million visitors a year.**

■ **The most-watched World Cup was in the United States in 1994. It had an average attendance of 70,000 fans a day.**

■ **The largest clock is in Mecca, Saudi Arabia. Each of its four faces is 43 meters (141 feet).**

■ **The busiest airport in the world is Hartsfield-Jackson International Airport, in Atlanta, Georgia, United States. It has more than 88 million passengers a year.**

■ ***Avatar* is the most popular movie ever. It has made more than $2.4 billion.**

■ **The longest nonstop flight is from New York to Singapore. It's 18.5 hours long.**

■ **Antarctica is the largest desert on earth at 14 million square kilometers (5.4 million square miles). It's also the coldest, windiest continent.**

■ **The highest price for a book at an auction is $11.5 million for *Birds of America* by John Audubon.**

■ **The strongest animal is the rhinoceros beetle. It can lift 850 times its own weight.**

Source: *The Top 10 of Everything;* www.extremescience.com

Which facts do you find surprising?
What's the tallest building in your country? the most popular city to visit?
  the busiest airport?

9 CONVERSATION *Distances and measurements*

A Listen and practice.

Scott: I'm going to Australia next year. Aren't you
  from Australia, Beth?
Beth: Actually, I'm from New Zealand.
Scott: Oh, I didn't know that. So what's it like there?
Beth: Oh, it's beautiful. There are lots of farms,
  and it's very mountainous.
Scott: Really? How high are the mountains?
Beth: Well, the highest one is Mount Cook.
  It's about 3,800 meters high.
Scott: Wow! So how far is New Zealand from Australia?
Beth: Well, I live in Auckland, and Auckland is
  about 2,000 kilometers from Sydney.
Scott: Maybe I should visit you next year, too!

Mount Cook

B Listen to the rest of the conversation.
What else is New Zealand famous for?

10 GRAMMAR FOCUS

Questions with how ▶

How far is New Zealand from Australia?	It's about 2,000 kilometers.	(1,200 miles)
How big is Singapore?	It's 710 square kilometers.	(274 square miles)
How high is Mount Cook?	It's 3,740 meters **high**.	(12,250 feet)
How deep is the Grand Canyon?	It's about 1,900 meters **deep**.	(6,250 feet)
How long is the Mississippi River?	It's about 5,970 kilometers **long**.	(3,710 miles)
How hot is Auckland in the summer?	It gets up to about 23° Celsius.	(74° Fahrenheit)
How cold is it in the winter?	It goes down to about 10° Celsius.	(50° Fahrenheit)

A Write the questions to these answers. Then practice with a partner.

1. A: .... ?
   B: Niagara Falls is 52 meters (170 feet) high.
2. A: .... ?
   B: California is about 403,970 square kilometers (155,973 square miles).
3. A: .... ?
   B: The Nile is 6,670 kilometers (4,145 miles) long.
4. A: .... ?
   B: Osaka is about 400 kilometers (250 miles) from Tokyo.
5. A: .... ?
   B: Mexico City gets up to about 28° Celsius (82° Fahrenheit) in the spring.

B GROUP WORK Think of five questions with *how* about places in your country or other countries you know. Ask and answer your questions.

11 WRITING An article

A Write an article to promote a place in your country. Describe a place in the list.

a beach
a desert
an island
a lake
a mountain
a river
a volcano
a waterfall

Web   Location   Photos   News   Ask

Jeju Island, South Korea

JEJU ISLAND

One of the most interesting places to go in South Korea is Jeju Island. Many people go there for its warm climate and beautiful beaches. I think one of the best places to visit there is Halla Mountain, or Halla-san. It's an old volcano and you can climb it in a day, but you should go early.

🅑 Tweet   🅕 Like

B PAIR WORK Read your partner's article. Ask questions to get more information.

Things You Can Do to Help the Environment

Look at the pictures. Which show environmental problems? Which show solutions?

CARS

Cars are getting bigger. SUVs—large, truck-like vehicles—are now the most popular cars in the United States. Bigger vehicles burn more gas and increase air pollution. So try to walk, bicycle, or use public transportation. If you drive a car, keep it tuned up. This saves gas and reduces pollution.

ENERGY

The biggest use of home energy is for heating and cooling. So turn up your air conditioner and turn down the heat, especially at night. Replace regular lightbulbs with bulbs that use less energy. And remember to turn lights off.

PRODUCTS

Each American throws away about 1.8 kilograms (4 pounds) of garbage every day. Most of it goes into landfills. Reduce waste before you buy by asking yourself: Do I need this? Is it something I can only use once? Buy products that you can use over and over again. And try to buy products made from recycled materials.

WATER

Showers use a lot of water. In one week, a typical American family uses as much water as a person drinks in three years! Buy a special "low-flow" showerhead or take shorter showers. This can cut water use in half. Also, fix any leaky faucets.

A Read the article. Where do you think it is from? Check (✓) the correct answer.

☐ a textbook ☐ an encyclopedia ☐ a magazine ☐ an advertisement

B Read these statements. Then write the advice from the article that each person should follow.

1. Stephanie always takes long showers in the morning. ....
2. In the winter, Ralph keeps the heat turned up all day. ....
3. Matt buys a newspaper every day, but never reads it. ....
4. Stuart drives to work, but his office is near his home. ....
5. Sheila leaves the lights on at home all the time. ....

C GROUP WORK What other ways do you know about to help the environment?

Units 13–14 Progress check

SELF-ASSESSMENT

How well can you do these things? Check (✓) the boxes.

I can	Very well	OK	A little
Say what I like and dislike (Ex. 1)	☐	☐	☐
Agree and disagree with other people (Ex. 1)	☐	☐	☐
Understand a variety of questions in a restaurant (Ex. 2)	☐	☐	☐
Order a meal in a restaurant (Ex. 3)	☐	☐	☐
Describe and compare things, people, and places (Ex. 4, 5)	☐	☐	☐
Ask questions about distances and measurements (Ex. 5)	☐	☐	☐

1 SURVEY *Food facts*

A Answer these questions. Write your responses under the column "My answers."

	My answers	Classmate's name
What food are you crazy about?	....	....
What food can't you stand?	....	....
Do you like vegetarian food?	....	....
Can you eat very rich food?	....	....
What restaurant do you like a lot?	....	....
How often do you go out to eat?	....	....

B CLASS ACTIVITY Go around the class. Find someone who has the same opinions or habits.

A: I'm crazy about Korean food.
B: I am, too./So am I. OR Oh, I'm not. I'm crazy about . . .

2 LISTENING *In a restaurant*

▶ Listen to six requests in a restaurant. Check (✓) the best response.

1. ☐ Yes. This way, please.
   ☐ Yes, please.

2. ☐ No, I don't.
   ☐ Yes, I'll have tea, please.

3. ☐ I'd like a steak, please.
   ☐ Yes, I would.

4. ☐ I'll have a cup of coffee.
   ☐ Italian, please.

5. ☐ Carrots, please.
   ☐ Yes, I will.

6. ☐ Yes, I'd like some water.
   ☐ No, I don't think so.

ROLE PLAY *What would you like?*

Student A: Imagine you are a server and Student B is a customer. Take his or her order and write it on the check.

Student B: Imagine you are a hungry customer and can order anything you like. Student A is a server. Order a meal.

Change roles and try the role play again.

Thank You! **TOTAL** _____

 SPEAKING *City quiz*

A PAIR WORK Write down six facts about your city using comparatives or superlatives. Then write six Wh-questions based on your facts.

> 1. The busiest street is Market Drive.
> What's the busiest street in our city?

B GROUP WORK Join another pair. Take turns asking the other pair your questions. How many can they answer correctly?

5 GAME *What's the question?*

A Think of three statements that can be answered with *how* questions or Wh-questions with comparatives and superlatives. Write each statement on a separate card.

B CLASS ACTIVITY Divide into Teams A and B. Shuffle the cards together. One student from Team A picks a card and reads it to a student from Team B. That student tries to make a question for it.

A: The Pacific Ocean is bigger than the Atlantic Ocean.
B: Which ocean is bigger, the Pacific or the Atlantic?

Keep score. The team with the most correct questions wins.

> *It's about four kilometers from my house to the school.*

> *The Pacific Ocean is bigger than the Atlantic Ocean.*

> *Ana has the longest hair in our class.*

WHAT'S NEXT?

Look at your Self-assessment again. Do you need to review anything?

15 I'm going to a soccer match.

1 **SNAPSHOT**

Making Excuses

Some common excuses for not accepting an invitation

I can't. I have to wash my hair.

- ☐ I'm busy that night.
- ☐ I can't find a babysitter.
- ☐ I'm not feeling well.
- ☐ I have to work then.
- ☐ I have class that night.
- ☐ My parents are visiting from out of town.
- ☐ I need to stay home with my new puppy.
- ☐ My favorite TV show is on that night.
- ☐ I have to get up early the next morning.

Sources: www.excuses.co.uk; interviews with people aged 18–45

Have you ever used any of these excuses? Have you ever heard any of them?
Which are good excuses and which are bad excuses? Check (✓) the good ones.
What other excuses can you make for not accepting an invitation?

2 **CONVERSATION** *Making plans*

A ▶ Listen and practice.

Lynn: Say, Miguel, what are you doing tonight? Do you want to go bowling?

Miguel: I'd love to, but I can't. I'm going to a soccer match with my brother.

Lynn: Oh, well, maybe some other time.

Miguel: Are you doing anything tomorrow? We could go then.

Lynn: Tomorrow sounds fine. I'm going to work until five.

Miguel: So let's go around six.

Lynn: OK. Afterward, maybe we can get some dinner.

Miguel: Sounds great.

B ▶ Listen to the rest of the conversation.
When are they going to have dinner? Who are they going to meet after dinner?

3 GRAMMAR FOCUS

Future with present continuous and be going to

With present continuous
What **are** you **doing** tonight?
   I**'m going** to a soccer match.
Are you **doing** anything tomorrow?
   No, I'm not.

With be going to + verb
What **is** she **going to do** tomorrow?
   She**'s going to work** until five.
Are they **going to go** bowling?
   Yes, they are.

Time expressions
tonight
tomorrow
on Friday
this weekend
next week

A Complete the invitations in column A with the present continuous used as future.
Complete the responses in column B with *be going to*.

A

1. What .... you .... (do) tonight?
   Would you like to go out?

2. .... you .... (do) anything on
   Friday night? Do you want to see a movie?

3. We .... (have) friends over for a
   barbecue on Sunday. Would you and your
   parents like to come?

4. .... you .... (stay) in town next
   weekend? Do you want to go for a hike?

B

a. I .... (be) here on Saturday, but not
   Sunday. Let's try and go on Saturday.

b. Well, my father .... (visit) my brother at
   college. But my mother and I .... (be)
   home. We'd love to come!

c. Sorry, I can't. I .... (work) overtime
   tonight. How about tomorrow night?

d. Can we go to a late show? I .... (stay)
   at the office till 7:00.

B Match the invitations in column A with the responses in column B. Then practice with a partner.

4 WORD POWER *Leisure activities*

A Complete the chart with words and phrases from the list.
Then add one more example to each category.

barbecue	bicycle race	picnic	singing contest
baseball game	birthday party	play	tennis match
beach party	dance performance	rock concert	volleyball tournament

Spectator sports	Friendly gatherings	Live performances
....	....	....
....	....	....
....	....	....
....	....	....
....	....	....

B **PAIR WORK** Are you going to do any of the activities in part A?
When are you doing them? Talk with a partner.

5

ROLE PLAY *Accept or refuse?*

Student A: Choose an activity from Exercise 4 and invite a partner to go with you. Be ready to say where and when the activity is.

> A: Say, are you doing anything on . . . ?
> Would you like to . . . ?

Student B: Your partner invites you out. Either accept the invitation and ask for more information, or say you can't go and give an excuse.

Accept	*Refuse*
B: OK. That sounds fun. Where is it?	B: Oh, I'm sorry, I can't. I'm . . .

Change roles and try the role play again.

INTERCHANGE 15 *Weekend plans*

Find out what your classmates are going to do this weekend.
Go to Interchange 15 on page 130.

CONVERSATION *Can I take a message?*

A ▶ Listen and practice.

Secretary: Good morning, Parker Industries.
  Mr. Kale: Hello. May I speak to Ms. Graham, please?
Secretary: I'm sorry. She's not in. Can I take a message?
  Mr. Kale: Yes, please. This is Mr. Kale.
Secretary: Is that G-A-L-E?
  Mr. Kale: No, it's K-A-L-E.
Secretary: All right.
  Mr. Kale: Please tell her our meeting is on Friday at 2:30.
Secretary: Friday at 2:30.
  Mr. Kale: And could you ask her to call me this afternoon? My number is (646) 555-4031.
Secretary: (646) 555-4031. Yes, Mr. Kale. I'll give Ms. Graham the message.
  Mr. Kale: Thank you. Good-bye.
Secretary: Good-bye.

B ▶ Listen to three other calls. Write down the callers' names.

8 GRAMMAR FOCUS

Messages with tell and ask ▶

Statement	Messages with a statement
The meeting is on Friday.	**Please tell her (that)** the meeting is on Friday.
	Could you tell her (that) the meeting is on Friday?
	Would you tell her (that) the meeting is on Friday?
Request	Messages with a request
Call me this afternoon.	**Please ask him to** call me this afternoon.
	Could you ask him to call me this afternoon?
	Would you ask him to call me this afternoon?

Unscramble these messages. Then compare with a partner.

1. tell / that / is / please / Ryan / the barbecue / on Saturday

   ....

2. call me / at 12:00 / you / Patrick / could /ask / to

   ....**?**

3. is / that / Amy / tonight / could / you / the dance performance / tell

   ....**?**

4. tell / is / Celia / in the park / would / you / that / the picnic

   ....**?**

5. meet me / to / you / would / Noriko / ask / at the stadium

   ....**?**

6. ask / to the rock concert / please / bring / Jason / to / the tickets

   ....

9 WRITING *Unusual favors*

A **PAIR WORK** Think of unusual messages for three people in your class.
Write a note to your partner asking him or her to pass on the messages.

Dear Rachel,

Could you tell Brian to wear two different color socks tomorrow?

Please tell Jeff that our class tomorrow is at midnight.

Would you ask Sun-hee to bring me a hamburger and french fries for breakfast tomorrow?

Thanks!

David

B **GROUP WORK** Compare your messages.
Which is the most unusual?

PRONUNCIATION *Reduction of* **could you** *and* **would you**

A ▶ Listen and practice. Notice how **could you** and **would you** are reduced in conversation.

[cʊdʒə]
Could you tell her the meeting is on Friday?

[wʊdʒə]
Would you ask him to call me this afternoon?

B **PAIR WORK** Practice these questions with reduced forms.

Could you tell them I'll be late?
Would you ask her to be on time?

Could you ask her to return my dictionary?
Would you tell him there's a picnic tomorrow?

11 **LISTENING** *Taking a message*

▶ Listen to telephone calls to Mr. Lin and Ms. Carson. Write down the messages.

1
To: Mr. _____

Date: _____ Time: _____

WHILE YOU WERE OUT

From: _____

of: City _____

Phone: _____ ext: _____

Message:
Call Mrs. _____
_____

Taken by: _____

2
To: Wendy _____

Date: _____ Time: _____

WHILE YOU WERE OUT

From: _____

of: _____ National _____

Phone: _____ ext: _____

Message:
_____
_____

Taken by: _____

12 **ROLE PLAY** *Who's calling?*

Student A: Call your friend Andrew to tell him this:

> There's a party at Ray's house on Saturday night.
> Ray's address is 414 Maple St., Apt. 202. Pick me up at 8:00 P.M.

Student B: Someone calls for your brother Andrew. He isn't in.
Take a message for him.

Change roles and try another role play.

Student A: You are a receptionist at Systex Industries. Someone calls for your boss, Ms. Park.
She isn't in. Take a message for her.

Student B: Call Ms. Park at Systex Industries to tell her this:

> You can't make your lunch meeting at 12:00. You want to meet at 12:30 at the same place
> instead. Call her to arrange the new time.

useful expressions
May I speak to . . . ?
Sorry, but . . . isn't here.
Can I leave a message?
Can I take a message?
I'll give . . . the message.

Cell Phone Etiquette

Scan the article. Is it OK to use a cell phone in a movie theater? in a restaurant? on the street?

What do these things have in common: a stranger's personal problems, details about a business meeting, the food in someone's refrigerator, someone's medical issues, and a private argument? These are all things you hear about when the people around you don't practice good cell phone etiquette!

Most people find cell phones a necessity in their day-to-day lives. But we've all sat next to someone talking too loudly, listening to loud music, or playing a loud beeping game on a cell phone. But a recent report shows that while most people are annoyed by cell phone rudeness, most admit to doing it, too. What can you do to practice better etiquette? Here are a few rules:

> **Off means off!** Respect the rules of restaurants and other public places. If a sign says "No cell phones," don't use your phone – for anything.

> **Keep private conversations private!** Speak softly and for a short time. Observe the 3-meter (10-feet) rule – stay away from other people.

> **Lights off, phone off!** Never take calls or send text messages in a theater, at the movies, or at a performance. Turn your phone or your ringer off.

> **Pay attention!** Talking or texting while driving is dangerous. Listening to music with headphones while driving is dangerous. Crossing the street while playing a game or checking your email is dangerous. You get the picture.

Cell phones have become mini-computers that people depend on 24 hours a day. But don't let yours become a nuisance – or a danger – to others! Next time you're getting ready to use yours, stop and consider the people around you.

A Read the article. Then complete the summary with information from the article.

Many people don't practice good cell phone .... They talk too .... , listen to .... music, or check their email while .... the street. To be a better cell phone user, follow a few simple rules. For example: Turn .... your phone in public places that don't allow cell phones; speak .... on phone calls; and don't talk, text, play games, or listen to music while .... or crossing the street.

B Check (✓) the statements the writer would probably agree with.

1. You should never use a cell phone in public.
2. Cell phone users are very rude people.
3. Turn off your cell phone if someone asks you to.
4. You can talk loudly if you're more than 3 meters away from someone.
5. It's OK to send text messages while driving a car.
6. You can use a cell phone at a dance performance if you speak quietly.
7. Don't play games on your phone in restaurants.
8. Don't check your email while crossing the street.

C **PAIR WORK** Do you agree with the writer's opinions? Why or why not?

16 A change for the better!

1 SNAPSHOT

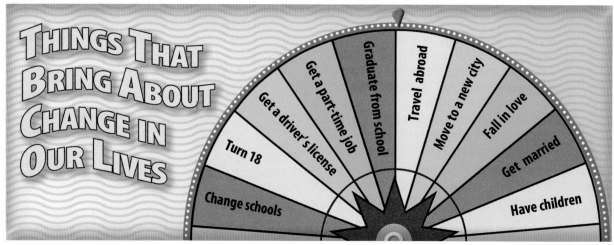

THINGS THAT BRING ABOUT CHANGE IN OUR LIVES

Turn 18
Change schools
Get a driver's license
Get a part-time job
Graduate from school
Travel abroad
Move to a new city
Fall in love
Get married
Have children

Source: Based on interviews with people between the ages of 16 and 50

Which of these events are the most important changes?
Have any of these things happened to you recently?
What other things bring about change in our lives?

2 CONVERSATION Catching up

A ▶ Listen and practice.

Diane: Hi, Kerry. I haven't seen you in ages. How have you been?
Kerry: Pretty good, thanks.
Diane: Are you still in school?
Kerry: No, not anymore. I graduated last year. And I got a job at Midstate Bank.
Diane: That's great news. You know, you look different. Have you changed your hair?
Kerry: Yeah, it's shorter. And I wear contacts now.
Diane: Well, you look fantastic!
Kerry: Thanks, so do you. And there's one more thing. Look! I got engaged.
Diane: Congratulations!

B ▶ Listen to the rest of the conversation. How has Diane changed?

3 GRAMMAR FOCUS

Describing changes

With the present tense
I'**m not** in school anymore.
I **wear** contacts now.

With the past tense
I **got** engaged.
I **moved** to a new place.

With the present perfect
I'**ve changed** jobs.
I'**ve fallen** in love.

With the comparative
My hair is **shorter** now.
My job is **less stressful**.

A How have you changed in the last five years?
Check (✓) the statements that are true for you.
If a statement isn't true, give the correct information.

- ⬜ 1. I've changed my hairstyle.
- ⬜ 2. I dress differently now.
- ⬜ 3. I've made some new friends.
- ⬜ 4. I got a pet.
- ⬜ 5. I've joined a club.
- ⬜ 6. I moved into my own apartment.
- ⬜ 7. I'm more outgoing than before.
- ⬜ 8. I'm not in high school anymore.
- ⬜ 9. My life is easier now.
- ⬜ 10. I got married.

B PAIR WORK Compare your responses in
part A. Have you changed in similar ways?

C GROUP WORK Write five sentences describing
other changes in your life. Then compare in groups.
Who in the group has changed the most?

4 LISTENING Memory lane

▶ Linda and Scott are looking through a photo album.
Listen to their conversation. How have they changed?
Write down three changes.

Changes
....
....
....

5 WORD POWER

A Complete the word map with phrases from the list. Then add two more examples to each category.

dye my hair
get a bank loan
get a credit card
grow a beard
improve my English vocabulary
learn a new sport
learn how to dance
open a savings account
pierce my ears
start a new hobby
wear contact lenses
win the lottery

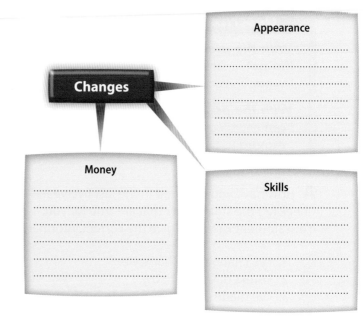

Changes

Appearance
....
....
....
....
....

Money
....
....
....
....
....

Skills
....
....
....
....
....

B **PAIR WORK** Have you changed in any of these areas? Tell your partner about a change in each category.

A: I opened a savings account last year. I've already saved $500.
B: I got my first credit card last month. Can I borrow … ?

6 CONVERSATION *Planning your future*

A ▶ Listen and practice.

Alex: So, what are you going to do after graduation, Susan?
Susan: Well, I've saved some money, and I think I'd really like to travel.
Alex: Lucky you. That sounds exciting!
Susan: Yeah. Then I plan to get a job and my own apartment.
Alex: Oh, you're not going to live at home?
Susan: No, I don't want to live with my parents – not after I start to work.
Alex: I know what you mean.
Susan: What about you, Alex? Any plans yet?
Alex: I'm going to get a job *and* live at home. I'm broke, and I want to pay off my student loan!

B ▶ Listen to the rest of the conversation. What kind of job does Alex want? Where would Susan like to travel?

7 GRAMMAR FOCUS

Verb + infinitive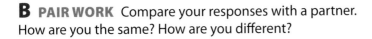

What **are** you **going to do** after graduation?
I**'m** (not) **going to get** a job right away.
I (don't) **plan to get** my own apartment.
I (don't) **want to live** with my parents.

I **hope to get** a new car.
I**'d like to travel** this summer.
I**'d love to move** to a new city.

A Complete these statements so that they are true for you.
Use information from the grammar box. Then add two more
statements of your own.

1. I .... travel abroad.
2. I .... live with my parents.
3. I .... get married.
4. I .... have a lot of children.
5. I .... make a lot of money!
6. I .... become very successful.
7. ....
8. ....

B **PAIR WORK** Compare your responses with a partner.
How are you the same? How are you different?

C **GROUP WORK** What are your plans for the future?
Take turns asking and answering these questions.

What are you going to do after this English course is over?
Do you plan to study here again next year?
What other languages would you like to learn?
What countries would you like to visit? Why?
Do you want to get a (new) job in a few years?
What kind of future do you hope to have?

8 PRONUNCIATION Vowel sounds /oʊ/ and /ʌ/

A ⊙ Many words spelled with *o* are pronounced /oʊ/ or /ʌ/.
Listen to the difference and practice.

/oʊ/ =	don't	smoke	go	loan	own	hope
/ʌ/ =	month	love	some	does	young	touch

B ⊙ Listen to these words. Check (✓) the correct pronunciation.

	both	cold	come	home	honey	money	mother	over
/oʊ/	☐	☐	☐	☐	☐	☐	☐	☐
/ʌ/	☐	☐	☐	☐	☐	☐	☐	☐

INTERCHANGE 16 *My possible future*

Imagine you could do anything, go anywhere, and meet anybody.
Go to Interchange 16 on page 131.

 SPEAKING *A class party*

A GROUP WORK Make plans for a class party.
Talk about these things and take notes.

Date	Transportation	Place	Food and drink
Time	Entertainment	Activities	Cost (if any)

A: When are we going to have our party?
B: I'd like to have it on Saturday.
C: That sounds fine. Let's plan to have it in the afternoon.
D: Can we start the party at noon?

B GROUP WORK Decide what each person is going
to bring to the party.

A: I can bring the drinks.
B: And I can bring some snacks.
C: Hey, why don't you bring
  your guitar?

WRITING *Party plans*

A GROUP WORK Work with your same group from Exercise 10.
As a group, write about your plans for the class party.

> Baseball Fun in the Sun!
> 1. Date and Time: We'd like to have our end-of-the-class party
>   next Saturday, on June 18th, from 12:00 – 4:00 p.m.
> 2. Place: We plan to meet at City Park near the baseball field.
>   If it rains, meet on Sunday at the same time and place.
> 3. Activities: We're going to play a class baseball game. The
>   game can start after lunch. Other activities are . . .

B CLASS ACTIVITY Present your plans to the class. Each person in
your group should present a different part. Then choose the best plan.

Setting Personal Goals

Look at the list in the article. Which of these areas of your life would you like to change or improve?

Ask any top athlete or successful businessperson and they will tell you the importance of setting goals. Goal setting can motivate you and give your life direction. It seems easy, right? Just write down a list of things you want to achieve and then do them. Well, it's not that easy!

Effective goal setting happens on several levels. First, you create a big picture of what you want to do with your life. At this point, you decide what large-scale goals you want to achieve. Second, you divide these into smaller and smaller tasks. Third, you put the smaller tasks into a rough time line. Finally, once you have your plan, you start working to achieve it.

How do you know what your large-scale goals are? These questions can help you get started.

- **Career**
  What level do you want to reach in your career?

- **Family**
  What kind of relationship do you want with the people in your family?

- **Community Service**
  How do you want to give back to your community?

- **Financial**
  How much money do you want to earn? How much do you want to save?

- **Creative**
  Do you want to achieve any artistic goals?

- **Physical**
  How will you stay in good physical shape throughout your life?

- **Education**
  What do you want to learn? How will you learn it?

- **Recreation**
  How do you want to enjoy yourself?

PROCESS

Write down your goals and think about them carefully. Are they realistic?

How important are they?

Rank them in order from most important to least important.

Then follow the process above to make your long-term plan. Remember, your goals can change with time. Look at them regularly and adjust them if necessary. And be sure your goals are things you hope to achieve, not things others want.

A Read the article. Who do you think the article was written for? Check (✓) the correct answer.

People who ...

☐ have very clear goals   ☐ are looking for direction   ☐ don't care about their future

B Answer these questions.

1. What kinds of people set personal goals? ....
2. Why do people set personal goals? ....
3. Why should you divide your goals into steps? ....
4. Why is it important to adjust your goals? ....

C **PAIR WORK** What is one of your personal goals? What steps will you take to achieve it?

Units 15–16 Progress check

SELF-ASSESSMENT

How well can you do these things? Check (✓) the boxes.

I can	Very well	OK	A little
Discuss future plans and arrangements (Ex. 1)	☐	☐	☐
Make and respond to invitations (Ex. 2)	☐	☐	☐
Understand and pass on telephone messages (Ex. 3)	☐	☐	☐
Ask and answer questions about changes in my life (Ex. 4)	☐	☐	☐
Describe personal goals (Ex. 5)	☐	☐	☐
Discuss and decide how to accomplish goals (Ex. 5)	☐	☐	☐

 1 DISCUSSION *The weekend*

A GROUP WORK Find out what your classmates are doing this weekend.
Ask for two details about each person's plans.

Name	Plans	Details
....	....	....
....	....	....
....	....	....

A: What are you going to do this weekend?
B: I'm seeing a rock concert on Saturday.
C: Which band are you going to see?

B GROUP WORK Whose weekend plans sound the best? Why?

2 ROLE PLAY *Inviting a friend*

Student A: Invite Student B to one of the events from
Exercise 1. Say where and when it is.
Student B: Student A invites you out. Accept and ask for
more information, or refuse and give an excuse.

Change roles and try the role play again.

3 LISTENING *Telephone messages*

 Listen to the telephone conversations. Write down the messages.

1
Message for: _____
Caller: _____
Message: _____
_____
_____
_____

2
Message for: _____
Caller: _____
Message: _____
_____
_____
_____

4 SURVEY *Changes*

A CLASS ACTIVITY Go around the class and find this information.
Write a classmate's name only once! Ask follow-up questions.

Find someone who	Name
1. got his or her hair cut last week	....
2. doesn't wear glasses anymore	....
3. has changed schools recently	....
4. goes out more often these days	....
5. got married last year	....
6. has started a new hobby	....
7. is happier these days	....
8. has gotten a part-time job recently	....

last week

this week

B CLASS ACTIVITY Compare your information.
Who in the class has changed the most?

5 SPEAKING *Setting goals*

Check (✓) the goals you have and add two more. Then choose one goal.
Plan how to accomplish it with a partner.

- ☐ own my own computer
- ☐ move to a new city
- ☐ have more free time
- ☐ have more friends
- ☐ get into a good school
- ☐ travel a lot more
- ☐ live a long time
- ☐ ....
- ☐ ....

A: I'd like to travel a lot more.
B: How are you going to do that?

WHAT'S NEXT?

Look at your Self-assessment again. Do you need to review anything?

Interchange activities

A **CLASS ACTIVITY** Go around the class and interview three classmates. Complete the chart.

Excuse me, Lady Gaga. Is Gaga your first name or your last name?

	Classmate 1	Classmate 2	Classmate 3
What's your first name?			
What's your last name?			
What city are you from?			
When's your birthday?			
What's your favorite color?			
What are your hobbies?			

B **GROUP WORK** Compare your information. Then discuss these questions.

Who...?

has an interesting first name   has the next birthday
has a common last name   likes black or white
is not from a big city   has an interesting hobby

A **CLASS ACTIVITY** Answer these questions about yourself. Then interview two classmates. Write their names and the times they do each thing.

What time do you . . . ?	Me	Name	Name
get up during the week			
get up on weekends			
have breakfast			
leave for school or work			
get home during the week			
have dinner			
go to bed during the week			
go to bed on weekends			

B **PAIR WORK** Whose schedule is similar to yours? Tell your partner.

A: Keiko and I have similar schedules. We both get up at 6:00 and have breakfast at 7:00.
B: I leave for work at 7:30, but Jeff leaves for school at . . .

useful expressions

We both . . . at . . .
We . . . at different times.
My schedule is different from my two classmates' schedules.

Student A

A You want to sell these things. Write your "asking price" for each item.

Student B

A You want to sell these things. Write your "asking price" for each item.

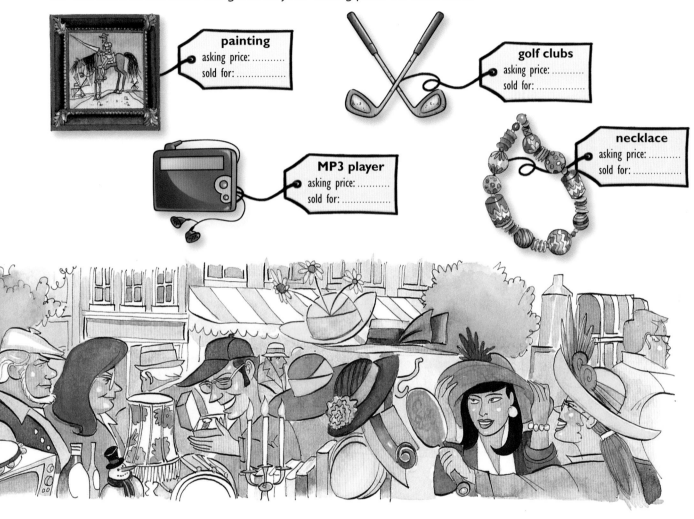

painting
asking price: ....
sold for: ....

golf clubs
asking price: ....
sold for: ....

MP3 player
asking price: ....
sold for: ....

necklace
asking price: ....
sold for: ....

Students A and B

B **PAIR WORK** Now choose three things you want to buy. Get the best price for each one. Then write what each item "sold for" on the price tag.

A: How much is the lamp?
B: It's only $30.
A: Wow! That's expensive!
B: Well, how about $25?
A: No. That's still too much. I'll give you $20 for it.
B: Sold! It's yours.

C **GROUP WORK** Compare your earnings in groups. Who made the most money at the flea market?

A Write two things you need to do this weekend. Include the times.

Saturday	Sunday
....	....
....	....

B Read the events page from your city's website. Choose three things you'd like to do.

On The Town

HOME
Log In
Register
Contact Us

Search the Calendar
What do you want to do?
GO

RESTAURANTS | LATE NIGHT | MUSIC | THEATER | MUSEUMS | OUTDOORS | KIDS | MOVIES | CALENDAR

TOP PICKS **What's on this weekend**

Saturday, May 21

Community Art Fair
See the work of local artists at the Community Art Fair! More than 200 artists, plus food, drinks, and music. Fun for the whole family!
11:00–5:00

Play Tennis!
Free tennis lessons for all ages. Central Park Tennis Courts. Bring a partner!
2:00–4:00

Bike Now's Ride Around the City
Once a year, this group organizes a bike ride around the city. Free food and drinks for cyclists from local restaurants.
Ride starts at 4:30.

Movies at Green Park
This Saturday's movie: *Avatar*. Bring your dinner, sit on the grass, and enjoy a movie under the stars.
Movie starts at 8:30. MORE

Sunday, May 22

Concerts on the River
Come hear your favorite music next to the White River. A different kind of music from a different country every week.
Concert starts at 1:00.

Chess in the Park
Bring a partner or find a partner at the city's biggest chess-a-thon. All levels and ages welcome. City Park, next to Park Café.
2:00–7:00

Free Tango Lessons
Learn to dance the tango! Live music and dancing. All levels. Beginners welcome. Center Street Activity Center.
5:30–7:00

City Baseball League
Green Park Team vs. the Lions. Come cheer for your favorite team! Come early to win prizes for the biggest fans!
Game at 7:30 MORE

C **GROUP WORK** Take turns inviting your classmates to the events. Say yes to one invitation and no to two invitations. Give a polite excuse.

A: Would you like to play tennis on Saturday? We can play from 2:00 to 4:00.
B: I'd like to, but I can't. I have to clean my room on Saturday afternoon.
A: Well, are you free in the morning?

A CLASS ACTIVITY Go around the class and find this information.
Write a classmate's name only once. Ask follow-up questions of your own.

Find someone	Name
1. who is an only child **"Do you have any brothers or sisters?"**	....
2. who has two brothers **"How many brothers do you have?"**	....
3. who has two sisters **"How many sisters do you have?"**	....
4. whose brother or sister is living abroad **"Are any of your brothers or sisters living abroad?"**	....
5. who lives with his or her grandparents **"Do you live with your grandparents?"**	....
6. who has a grandparent still working **"Is your grandmother or grandfather still working?"**	....
7. who has a family member with an unusual job **"Does anyone in your family have an unusual job?"**	....
8. whose mother or father is studying English **"Is either of your parents studying English?"**	....

B GROUP WORK Compare your information.

A **CLASS ACTIVITY** Does anyone in your class do these things?
How often and how well? Go around the class and find one person
for each activity.

	Name	How often?	How well?
dance	....	....	....
play an instrument	....	....	....
sing	....	....	....
act	....	....	....
tell jokes	....	....	....
do gymnastics	....	....	....
do magic tricks	....	....	....

A: Do you dance?
B: Yes, I do.
A: How often do you go dancing?
B: Every weekend.
A: Really? And how well do you dance?

B **GROUP WORK** Imagine there's a talent show this weekend.
Who do you want to enter? Choose three people from your class.
Explain your choices.

A: Let's enter Adam in the talent show.
B: Why Adam?
A: Because he dances very well.
C: Yes, he does. And Yvette is very good at playing the guitar.
    Let's enter her, too!

GROUP WORK Play the board game. Follow these instructions.

1. Use small pieces of paper with your initials on them as markers.
2. Take turns by tossing a coin: If the coin lands face up, move two spaces. If the coin lands face down, move one space.
3. When you land on a space, answer the question. Answer any follow-up questions.
4. If you land on "Free question," another player asks you any question.

A: I'll go first. Last night, I met my best friend.
B: Oh, yeah? Where did you go?
A: We went to the movies.

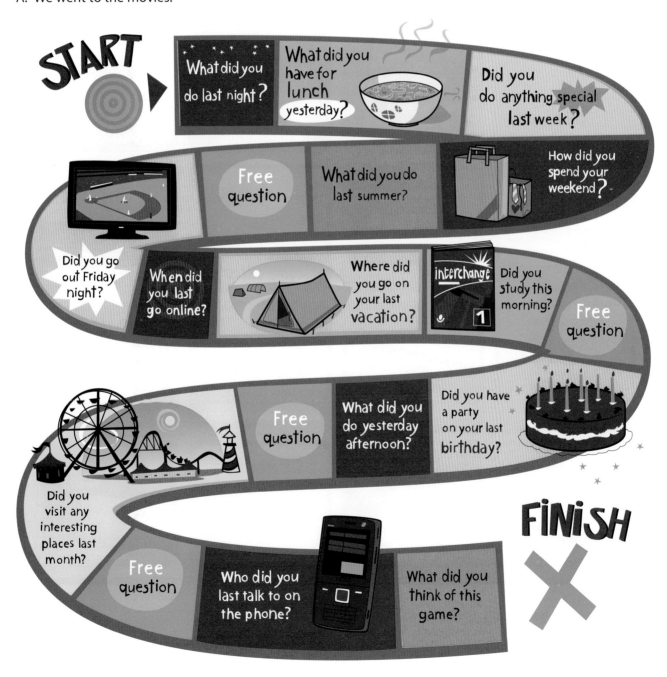

CLASS ACTIVITY Play a guessing game. Follow these instructions.

1. Get into two teams, A and B. One student from each team goes to the front of the class.
2. These two students choose a location and give four clues, using *There is/are* plus a quantifier.
3. The first student to guess the location correctly joins his or her teammate at the front.
4. The new student chooses a different location and gives clues. His or her team answers.
5. The first team with all of its members in the front wins.

A: There isn't any food in this place. There's a lot of coffee. There are a few computers. There are many emails. Where am I?
B: In an Internet café!
A: Correct! Now you come to the front.

Student A

A PAIR WORK How many differences can you find between your picture here and your partner's picture? Ask questions like these to find the differences.

How many people are standing / sitting / wearing . . . / holding a drink? Who?
What color is . . . 's T-shirt / sweater / hair?
Does . . . wear glasses / have a beard / have long hair?
What does . . . look like?

B CLASS ACTIVITY How many differences are there in the pictures?

"In picture 1, Dave's T-shirt is . . . . In picture 2, it's . . ."

Student B

A **PAIR WORK** How many differences can you find between your picture here and your partner's picture? Ask questions like these to find the differences.

How many people are standing / sitting / wearing . . . / holding a drink? Who?
What color is . . . 's T-shirt / sweater / hair?
Does . . . wear glasses / have a beard / have long hair?
What does . . . look like?

B **CLASS ACTIVITY** How many differences are there in the pictures?

"In picture 1, Dave's T-shirt is . . . . In picture 2, it's . . ."

A **PAIR WORK** What kind of lifestyle does your partner have? Interview him or her. Write the number of points using this scale.

never = 1 point
1–3 times = 2 points

4–7 times = 3 points
8 or more times = 4 points

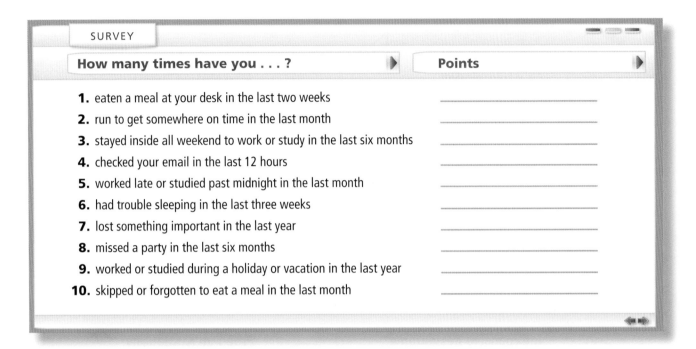

SURVEY

How many times have you . . . ?	Points
1. eaten a meal at your desk in the last two weeks	
2. run to get somewhere on time in the last month	
3. stayed inside all weekend to work or study in the last six months	
4. checked your email in the last 12 hours	
5. worked late or studied past midnight in the last month	
6. had trouble sleeping in the last three weeks	
7. lost something important in the last year	
8. missed a party in the last six months	
9. worked or studied during a holiday or vacation in the last year	
10. skipped or forgotten to eat a meal in the last month	

B **GROUP WORK** Add up your partner's points. Tell the group what your partner's lifestyle is like and why.

10–19 = You are a well-balanced person who knows how to relax, breathe deeply, and stop and smell the roses. Keep it up!

20–29 = You're doing OK, but you need to be careful. Continue to take time to do the things that are important to you.

30–40 = You are overdoing it! Your life is too busy and fast-paced. You need to slow down and relax more.

"Pedro is overdoing it. His lifestyle is too busy and fast-paced. He never goes to parties, and he often studies past midnight. And he sometimes forgets to eat. He also . . ."

C **CLASS ACTIVITY** Do you think your partner needs to change his or her lifestyle? In what way?

"I think Pedro needs to slow down a little. He needs to try to eat regular meals and . . ."

A Where can you get information about a city? buy souvenirs? see historical sights? Complete the city guide with information about a city of your choice.

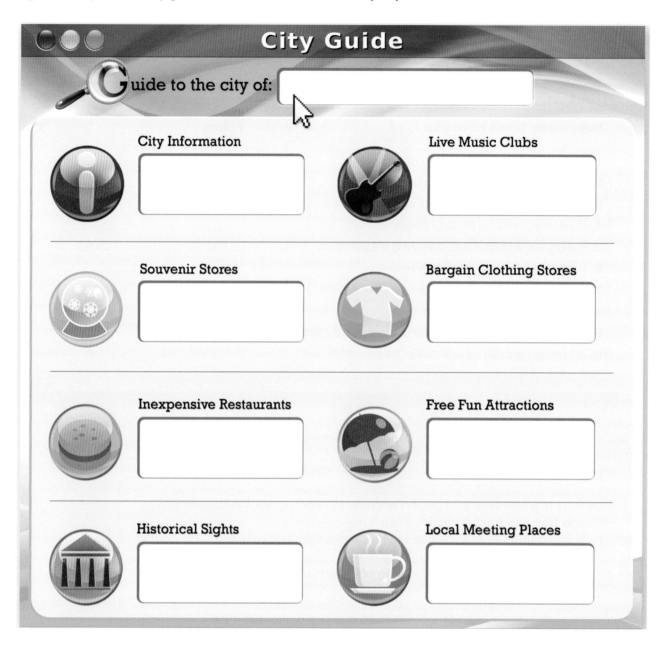

B **GROUP WORK** Compare your city guide in groups. Ask these questions and questions of your own. Add any additional or interesting information to your guide.

Where can you get information about your city?
Where's a good place to buy souvenirs?
Where's an inexpensive place to eat?
What historical sights should you visit?
Where's the best place to hear live music?
Where's a cheap place to shop for clothes?
What fun things can you do for free?
Where's a popular place to meet?

A GROUP WORK Play the board game. Follow these instructions.

1. Use small pieces of paper with your initials on them as markers.
2. Take turns by tossing a coin:
   If the coin lands face up, move two spaces.
   If the coin lands face down, move one space.
3. When you land on a space, ask two others in your group for advice.

A: I have a terrible headache. Akira, what's your advice?
B: Well, it's important to get a lot of rest.
A: Thanks. What about you, Jason? What do you think?
C: You should take two aspirin. That always works for me.

useful expressions
You should . . .
You could . . .
It's a good idea to . . .
It's important to . . .
I think it's useful to . . .

B CLASS ACTIVITY Who gave the best advice in your group? Tell the class.

A GROUP WORK Imagine you are opening a new restaurant. Create a menu of dishes you'd like to offer. Then write the prices.

B GROUP WORK Choose a name for your restaurant. Write it at the top of the menu.

C CLASS ACTIVITY Compare your menus. Which group has . . . ?

   the most interesting menu
   the most typical menu
   the healthiest menu
   the cheapest prices
   the best name for a restaurant

A PAIR WORK Take turns asking and answering these questions.
Check (✓) the answer you think is correct for each question.

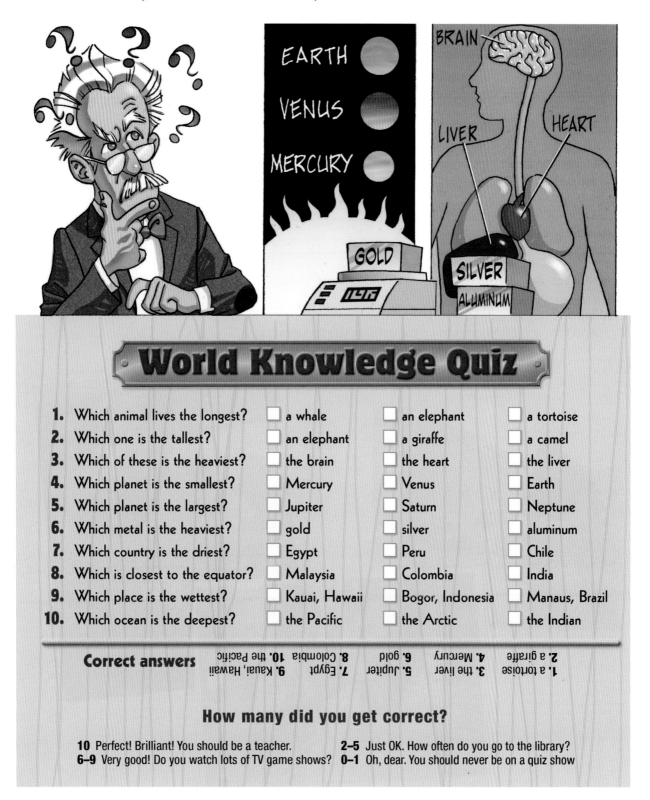

World Knowledge Quiz

1.	Which animal lives the longest?	☐ a whale	☐ an elephant	☐ a tortoise
2.	Which one is the tallest?	☐ an elephant	☐ a giraffe	☐ a camel
3.	Which of these is the heaviest?	☐ the brain	☐ the heart	☐ the liver
4.	Which planet is the smallest?	☐ Mercury	☐ Venus	☐ Earth
5.	Which planet is the largest?	☐ Jupiter	☐ Saturn	☐ Neptune
6.	Which metal is the heaviest?	☐ gold	☐ silver	☐ aluminum
7.	Which country is the driest?	☐ Egypt	☐ Peru	☐ Chile
8.	Which is closest to the equator?	☐ Malaysia	☐ Colombia	☐ India
9.	Which place is the wettest?	☐ Kauai, Hawaii	☐ Bogor, Indonesia	☐ Manaus, Brazil
10.	Which ocean is the deepest?	☐ the Pacific	☐ the Arctic	☐ the Indian

Correct answers **1.** a tortoise **2.** a giraffe **3.** the liver **4.** Mercury **5.** Jupiter **6.** gold **7.** Egypt **8.** Colombia **9.** Kauai, Hawaii **10.** the Pacific

How many did you get correct?

10 Perfect! Brilliant! You should be a teacher.   **2–5** Just OK. How often do you go to the library?
6–9 Very good! Do you watch lots of TV game shows?   **0–1** Oh, dear. You should never be on a quiz show

B PAIR WORK Create your own quiz. Write 3 to 5 questions.
Then ask the questions to another pair.

A CLASS ACTIVITY What are your classmates' plans for the weekend?
Go around the class and find people who are going to do these things.
For each question, ask for further information.

Find someone who is going to . . .	Name	Notes
go out of town	....	....
meet friends	....	....
stay out late	....	....
visit relatives	....	....
go to a party	....	....
see a live performance	....	....
play video games	....	....
study for a test	....	....
exercise	....	....
buy something for someone	....	....

A: Omar, are you going to go out of town this weekend?
B: Yes, I am.
A: What are you going to do?
B: My friend Tom and I are going to go camping in the mountains.

B PAIR WORK Compare your information with a partner.
Who is going to do something fun? physical? serious?

A Complete this chart with information about yourself.

My possible future	
What are two things you plan to do next year?	....
	....
What are two things you aren't going to do next year?	....
	....
What is something you hope to buy in the next year?	....
What would you like to change about yourself?	....
Where would you like to visit someday?	....
What city would you like to live in someday?	....
What kind of job would you like to have?	....
What career goals do you hope to achieve?	....
What famous person would you like to meet?	....

B **GROUP WORK** Compare your information in groups.
Be prepared to explain the future you have planned.

A: What are two things you plan to do next year?
B: Well, I'm going to take a cooking class, and I'm also going to go to Italy.
C: Oh, really? What part of Italy are you going to visit?
B: I'm not sure yet! What about you? What are two things you plan to do next year?

Grammar plus

Unit 1

1 Statements with *be*; possessive adjectives (page 3)

▶ Don't confuse contractions of *be* with possessive adjectives: **You're** a student. **Your** class is English 1. (NOT: ~~You're class is English 1.~~) **He's** my classmate. **His** name is Roberto. (NOT: ~~He's name is Roberto.~~)

Circle the correct words.

1. This **is** / **are** Delia Rios. **She's** / **Her** a new student from Peru.
2. My name **am** / **is** Sergio. **I'm** / **He's** from Brazil.
3. My brother and I **is** / **are** students here. **Our** / **We're** names are Dave and Jeff.
4. **He's** / **His** Yoshi. **He's** / **His** 19 years old.
5. **They're** / **Their** in my English class. **It's** / **Its** a big class.

2 Wh-questions with *be* (page 4)

▶ Use *What* to ask about things: **What's** in your bag? Use *Where* to ask about places: **Where's** your friend from? Use *Who* to ask about people: **Who's** your teacher? Use *What . . . like?* to ask for a description: **What's** your friend **like**?

Match the questions with the answers.

1. Who's that? ...f...
2. Where's your teacher? ....
3. What are your friends like? ....
4. Where's she from? ....
5. Who are they? ....
6. What's his name? ....

a. They're really nice.
b. She's from Japan.
c. They're my brother and sister.
d. His name is Carlos.
e. He's in class.
f. That's our new classmate.

3 Yes/No questions and short answers with *be* (page 5)

▶ Use short answers to answer yes/no questions. Don't use contractions with short answers with *Yes*: **Are you** from Mexico? Yes, **I am**. (NOT: ~~Yes, I'm.~~)

Complete the conversations.

1. A: _Are they_ in your class?
   B: No, ... They're in English 2.
2. A: Hi! .... in this class?
   B: Yes, ... I'm a new student here.
3. A: .... from the United States?
   B: No, ... We're from Montreal, Canada.
4. A: Hi, Sonia. .... free?
   B: No, ... I'm on my way to class.
5. A: That's the new student. .... from Puerto Rico?
   B: No, ... He's from Costa Rica.
6. A: .... from Thailand?
   B: Yes, ... She's from Bangkok.

Unit 2

1 Simple present Wh-questions and statements (page 10)

> **Statements**
> ▶ Verbs with he/she/it end in –s: He/She **walks** to school. BUT I/You/We/They **walk** to school.
> ▶ *Have, go,* and *do* are irregular with he/she/it: She **has** a class at 1:00. He **goes** to school at night. She **does** her homework before school.

> **Wh-questions**
> ▶ Use *does* in questions with he/she/it and *do* with all the others: Where *does* he/she/it live? Where *do* I/you/we/they live?
> ▶ Don't add –s to the verb: Where does she **live**? (NOT: ~~Where does she lives?~~)

Complete the conversations with the correct form of the verbs in parentheses.

1. A: I ...._have_........ (have) good news! Dani .... (have) a new job.
   B: How .... she .... (like) it?
   A: She .... (love) it. The hours are great.
   B: What time .... she .... (start)?
   A: She .... (start) at nine and .... (finish) at five.
2. A: What .... you .... (do)?
   B: I'm a teacher.
   A: What .... you .... (teach)?
   B: I .... (teach) Spanish and English.
   A: Really? My sister .... (teach) English, too.

2 Time expressions (page 12)

> ▶ Use *in* with *the morning/afternoon/evening*. Us *at* with *night*: He goes to school **in** the afternoon and works **at** night. BUT: **on** Friday night.
> ▶ Use *at* with clock times: She gets up **at** 7:00.
> ▶ Use *on* with days: He gets up early **on** weekdays. She has class **on** Mondays.

Complete the conversation with time expressions from the box. You can use some words more than once.

at	early	in	on	until

A: How's your new job?
B: I love it, but the hours are difficult. I start work .... 7:30 A.M., and I work .... 3:30.
A: That's interesting! I work the same hours, but I work .... night. I start .... 7:30 .... the evening and finish .... 3:30 .... the morning.
B: Wow! What time do you get up?
A: Well, I get home .... 4:30 and go to bed .... 5:30. And I sleep .... 2:00. But I only work .... weekends, so it's OK. What about you?
B: Oh, I work .... Monday, Wednesday, and Friday. And I get up .... – around 6:00 A.M.

Unit 3

1 Demonstratives; *one, ones* (page 17)

> ▶ With singular nouns, use *this* for a thing that is nearby and *that* for a thing that is not nearby: How much is **this** cap here? How much is **that** cap over there?
> ▶ With plural nouns, use *these* for things that are nearby and *those* for things that are not nearby: How much are **these** earrings here? How much are **those** earrings over there?
> ▶ Use *one* to replace a singular noun: I like the red <u>hat</u>. → I like the red **one**. Use *ones* to replace plural nouns: I like the green <u>bags</u>. → I like the green **ones**.

Circle the correct words.

1. A: Excuse me. How much are **this / these** shoes?
   B: **It's / They're** $279.
   A: And how much is **this / that** bag over there?
   B: **It's / They're** only $129.
   A: And are the two gray **one / ones** $129, too?
   B: No. **That / Those** are only $119.
   A: Oh! **This / That** store is really expensive.
2. A: Can I help you?
   B: Yes, please. I really like **these / those** jeans over there. How much **is it / are they**?
   A: Which **one / ones**? Do you mean **this / these**?
   B: No, the black **one / ones**.
   A: Let me look. Oh, **it's / they're** $35.99.
   B: That's not bad. And how much is **this / that** sweater here?
   A: **It's / They're** only $9.99.

2 Preferences; comparisons with adjectives (page 20)

> ▶ With adjectives of one or two syllables, add *–er* to form the comparative: cheap → cheaper; nice → nicer; pretty → prettier; big → bigger.
> ▶ With adjectives of three or more syllables, use *more* + adjective to form the comparative: expensive → more expensive.

A Write the comparatives of these adjectives.

1.	attractive	....more attractive....	5. interesting	....
2.	boring	....	6. reasonable	....
3.	exciting	....	7. sad	....
4.	friendly	....	8. warm	....

B Answer the questions. Use the words in parentheses in your answer. Then write another sentence with the second word.

1. Which pants do you prefer, the cotton ones or the wool ones? (wool / attractive)
   I prefer the wool ones. They're more attractive than the cotton ones
2. Which ring do you like better, the gold one or the silver one? (silver / interesting)
   ....
3. Which one do you prefer, the silk jacket or the wool jacket? (silk / pretty)
   ....
4. Which ones do you like more, the black shoes or the purple ones? (purple / exciting)
   ....

Unit 4

1 Simple present questions; short answers (page 23)

> ▶ Use *do* + base form for yes/no questions and short answers with I/you/we/they:
> **Do** I/you/we/they **like** rock? Yes, I/you/we/they **do**. No, I/you/we/they **don't**.
> ▶ Use *does* in yes/no questions and short answers with he/she/it: **Does** he/she **like**
> rock? Yes, he/she **does**. No, he/she **doesn't**.
> ▶ Use *don't* and *doesn't* + base form for negative statements: I **don't like** horror
> movies. He **doesn't like** action movies.
> ▶ Remember: Don't add *–s* to the base form: Does she **like** rock? (NOT: ~~Does she~~
> ~~likes rock?~~)
> ▶ Subject pronouns (*I, you, he, she, it, we, they*) usually come before a verb. Object
> pronouns (*me, you, him, her, it, us, them*) usually come after a verb: He likes **her**, but
> she doesn't like **him**.

A Complete the questions and short answers.

1. A: *Do you play* (play) a musical instrument?
   B: Yes, ...*I do*............ . I play the guitar.
2. A: .... (like) Taylor Swift?
   B: No, ... Joe doesn't like country music.
3. A: .... (like) talk shows?
   B: Yes, ... Lisa is a big fan of them.
4. A: .... (watch) the news on TV?
   B: Yes, ... Kevin and I watch the news every night.
5. A: .... (like) hip-hop?
   B: No, ... But I love R&B.
6. A: .... (listen to) jazz?
   B: No, ... But my parents listen to a lot of classical music.

B Complete the sentences with object pronouns.

1. We don't listen to hip-hop because we really don't like ....*it*.... .
2. We love your voice. Please sing for ....
3. These sunglasses are great. Do you like .... ?
4. Who is that man? Do you know .... ?
5. Beth looks great in green. It's a really good color for ....

2 *Would*; verb + *to* + verb (page 26)

> ▶ Don't use a contraction in affirmative short answers with *would*: **Would** you **like to**
> **go to** the game? Yes, I **would**. (NOT: ~~Yes, I'd.~~)

Unscramble the questions and answers to complete the conversation.

A: tonight   to see   would you like   with me   a movie
.... ?

B: I would.   yes,   what   to see   would you like
.... ?

A: the new Halle Berry movie   to see   I'd like
....

B: OK. That's a great idea!

Unit 5

1 Present continuous (page 32)

> ▶ Use the present continuous to talk about actions that are happening now: What **are** you **doing (these days)**? I**'m studying** English.
> ▶ The present continuous is present of *be* + *-ing*. For verbs ending in *e*, drop the *e* and add *–ing*: have → having, live → living.
> ▶ For verbs ending in vowel + consonant, double the consonant and add *–ing*: sit → sitting.

Write questions with the words in parentheses and the present continuous. Then complete the responses with short answers or the verbs in the box.

> live   study   take   ✓ teach   work

1. A: (what / your sister / do / these days) What's your sister doing these days?
   B: She's teaching English.
   A: Really? (she / live / abroad) ....
   B: Yes, ... She .... in South Korea
2. A: (how / you / spend / your summer) ....
   B: I .... part-time. I .... two classes also.
   A: (what / you / take) ....
   B: My friend and I .... photography and Japanese. We like our classes a lot.

2 Quantifiers (page 34)

> ▶ Use *a lot of*, *all*, *few*, *nearly all* before plural nouns: **A lot of/All/Few/Nearly all** families are small. Use *no one* before a verb: **No one** gets married before the age of 18.
> ▶ *Nearly all* means "almost all."

Read the sentences about the small town of Monroe. Rewrite the sentences using the quantifiers in the box. Use each quantifier only once.

> a lot of   all   few   nearly all   ✓ no one

1. In Monroe, 0% of the people drive before the age of 16.
   In Monroe, no one drives before the age of 16.
2. Ninety-eight percent of students finish high school.
   ....
3. One hundred percent of children start school by the age of six.
   ....
4. Eighty-nine percent of couples have more than one child.
   ....
5. Twenty-three percent of families have more than four children.
   ....

Unit 6

1 Adverbs of frequency (page 37)

> ▶ Adverbs of frequency (*always, almost always, usually, often, sometimes, hardly ever, almost never, never*) usually come before the main verb: She **never plays** tennis. I **almost always eat** breakfast. BUT Adverbs of frequency usually come after the verb *be*: I**'m always** late.
> ▶ *Usually* and *sometimes* can begin a sentence: **Usually** I walk to work. **Sometimes** I exercise in the morning.
> ▶ Some frequency expressions usually come at the end of a sentence: *every day, once a week, twice a month, three times a year*: Do you exercise **every day**? I exercise **three times a week**.

Put the words in order to make questions. Then complete the answers with the words in parentheses.

1. you   what   weekends   usually   do   do   on
   Q: *What do you usually do on weekends?* ....
   A: I .... (often / play sports)
2. ever   you   go jogging   do   with a friend
   Q: ....
   A: No, ... (always / alone)
3. you   play   do   tennis   how often
   Q: ....
   A: I .... (four times a week)
4. do   you   what   in the evening   usually   do
   Q: ....
   A: My family and I .... (almost always / watch TV)
5. go   how often   you   do   to the gym
   Q: ....
   A: I .... (never)

2 Questions with *how*; short answers (page 40)

> ▶ Don't confuse *good* and *well*. Use the adjective *good* with *be* and the adverb *well* with other verbs: How **good** are you at soccer? BUT How **well** do you play soccer?

Complete the questions with *How* and a word from the box. Then match the questions and the answers.

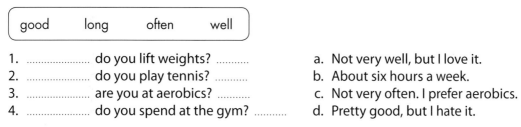

good   long   often   well

1. .... do you lift weights? ....   a. Not very well, but I love it.
2. .... do you play tennis? ....   b. About six hours a week.
3. .... are you at aerobics? ....   c. Not very often. I prefer aerobics.
4. .... do you spend at the gym? ....   d. Pretty good, but I hate it.

Unit 7

1 Simple past (page 45)

> ▶ Use *did* with the base form – not the past form – of the main verb in questions: How **did** you **spend** the weekend? (NOT: ~~How did you spent . . .?~~)
> ▶ Use *didn't* with the base form in negative statements: We **didn't go** shopping. (NOT: . . . ~~we didn't went shopping.~~)

Complete the conversation.

A: ....Did.... you ..have... (have) a good weekend?

B: Yes, I .... I .... (have) a great time. My sister and I .... (go) shopping on Saturday. We .... (spend) all day at the mall.

A: .... you .... (buy) anything special?

B: I .... (buy) a new laptop. And I .... (get) some new clothes, too.

A: Lucky you! What clothes .... you .... (buy)?

B: Well, I .... (need) some new boots. I .... (find) some great ones at Luff's Department Store.

A: What about you? What .... you .... (do) on Saturday?

B: I .... (not do) anything special. I .... (stay) home and .... (work) around the house. Oh, but I .... (see) a really good movie on TV. And then I .... (make) dinner with my mother. I actually .... (enjoy) the day.

2 Past of *be* (page 47)

> ▶ Present   Past
>   am/is → **was**
>   are   → **were**

Rewrite the sentences. Find another way to write each sentence using *was, wasn't, were,* or *weren't* and the words in parentheses.

1. Tony didn't come to class yesterday. (in class)
   Tony wasn't in class yesterday. ....

2. He worked all day. (at work)
   ....

3. Tony and his co-workers worked on Saturday, too. (at work)
   ....

4. They didn't go to work on Sunday. (at work)
   ....

5. Did Tony stay home on Sunday? (at home)
   ....

6. Where did Tony go on Sunday? (on Sunday)
   ....

7. He and his brother went to a baseball game. (at a baseball game)
   ....

8. They stayed at the park until 7:00. (at the park)
   ....

Unit 8

1 There is, there are; one, any, some (page 51)

> ▶ Don't use a contraction in a short answer with *Yes*: Is there a hotel near here? Yes, **there is**. (NOT: ~~Yes, there's.~~)
> ▶ Use *some* in affirmative statements and *any* in negative statements: There are **some** grocery stores in my neighborhood, but there aren't **any** restaurants. Use *any* in most questions: Are there **any** nice stores around here?

Complete the conversations. Circle the correct words.

1. A: **Is / Are** there any supermarkets in this neighborhood?
   B: No, there **isn't / aren't**, but there are **one / some** on Main Street.
   A: And **is / are** there a post office near here?
   B: Yes, **there's / there is**. It's across from the bank.
2. A: **Is / Are** there a gas station around here?
   B: Yes, **there's / there are** one behind the shopping center.
   A: Great! And are there **a / any** coffee shops nearby?
   B: Yes, there's a good **one / some** in the shopping center.

2 Quantifiers; how many and how much (page 54)

> ▶ Use *a lot* with both count and noncount nouns: Are there many traffic lights on First Avenue? Yes, there are **a lot**. Is there much traffic? Yes, there's **a lot**.
> ▶ Use *any* – not *none* – in negative statements: How much traffic is there on your street? There **isn't any**. = There**'s none**. (NOT: ~~There isn't none.~~)
> ▶ Use *How many* with count nouns: **How many books** do you have?
> ▶ Use *How much* with noncount nouns: **How much traffic** is there?

A Complete the conversations. Circle the correct words.

1. A: Is there **many / much** traffic in your city?
   B: Well, there's **a few / a little**.
2. A: Are there **many / much** public telephones around here?
   B: No, there aren't **many / none**.
3. A: **How many / How much** restaurants are there in your neighborhood?
   B: There **is / are** a lot.
4. A: **How many / How much** noise **is / are** there in your city?
   B: There's **much / none**. It's very quiet.

B Write questions with the words in parentheses. Use *much* or *many*.

1. A: Is there much pollution in your neighborhood? .... (pollution)
   B: No, there isn't. My neighborhood is very clean.
2. A: .... (parks)
   B: Yes, there are. They're great for families.
3. A: .... (crime)
   B: There's none. It's a very safe part of the city.
4. A: .... (laundromats)
   B: There aren't any. A lot of people have their own washing machines.

Unit 9

1 Describing people (page 59)

> ▶ Use *have* or *is* to describe eye and hair color: I **have** brown hair. = My hair **is** brown.
> He **has** blue eyes. = His eyes **are** blue.
> ▶ Don't confuse *How* and *What* in questions: **How** tall are you? (NOT: ~~What tall are you?~~) **What** color is your hair? (NOT: ~~How color is your hair?~~)

Unscramble the questions. Then write answers using the phrases in the box.

blond	brown eyes	contact lenses
✓ tall and good-looking	5 feet 11	26 – two years older than me

A: brother   like   look   what   your   does
   What does your brother look like?
B: *He's tall and good-looking.*
A: tall   is   how   he
   ....
B: ....
A: he   does   glasses   wear
   ....
B: ....
A: what   hair   color   his   is
   ....
B: ....
A: he   does   blue   have   eyes
   ....
B: ....
A: old   he   how   and   is
   ....
B: ....

2 Modifiers with participles and prepositions (page 62)

> ▶ Don't use a form of *be* in modifiers with participles: Sylvia is the woman **standing** near the window. (NOT: ~~Sylvia is the woman is standing near the window.~~)

Rewrite the conversations. Use the words in parentheses and *one* or *ones*.

1. A: Who's Carla?   A: *Which one is Carla?* .... (which)
   B: She's the woman in the red dress.   B: .... (wearing)
2. A: Who are your neighbors?   A: .... (which)
   B: They're the people with the baby.   B: .... (walking)
3. A: Who's Jeff?   A: .... (which)
   B: He's the man wearing glasses.   B: .... (with)

Unit 10

1 Present perfect; *already, yet* (page 65)

> ▶ Use the present perfect for actions that happened some time in the past.
> ▶ Use *yet* in questions and negative statements: Have you checked your email **yet**?
> No, I haven't turned on my computer **yet**. Use *already* in affirmative statements:
> I've **already** checked my email.

A Complete the conversations with the present perfect of the verbs in parentheses
and short answers.

1. A: ....Has....... Leslie .....called..... (call) you lately?
   B: No, she .... (not call) me, but I .... (get) some emails from her.
2. A: .... you and Jan .... (have) lunch yet?
   B: No, we .... We're thinking of going to Tony's. .... you
   .... (try) it yet? Come with us.
   A: Thanks. I .... (not eat) there yet, but I .... (hear) it's pretty good.

B Look at things Matt said. Put the adverb in the correct place in the second sentence.

1. I'm very hungry. I haven't eaten. (yet)   *yet*
2. I don't need any groceries. I've gone shopping. (already)
3. What have you done? Have you been to the zoo? (yet)
4. I called my parents before dinner. I've talked to them. (already)

2 Present perfect vs. simple past (page 66)

> ▶ Don't mention a specific time with the present perfect: I've **been** to a jazz club.
> Use the simple past to say when a past action happened: I **went** to a jazz club
> **last night**.

Complete the conversation using the present perfect or the simple past of the verbs in
parentheses and short answers.

1. A: ....Did.... you ....see.... (see) the game last night? I really .... (enjoy) it.
   B: Yes, I .... It .... (be) an amazing game. .... you ever .... (go) to a game?
   A: No, I .... I .... never .... (be) to the stadium. But I'd love to go!
   Maybe we can go to a game next year.
2. A: .... you ever .... (be) to Franco's Restaurant?
   B: Yes, I .... My friend and I .... (eat) there last weekend. How about you?
   A: No, I .... But I .... (hear) it's very good.
   B: Oh, yes – it's excellent!

3 *For* and *since* (page 67)

> ▶ Use *for* + a period of time to describe how long a present condition has been true:
> We've been in New York **for two months**. (= We arrived two months ago.)
> ▶ Use *since* + a point in time to describe when a present condition started: We've
> been here **since August**. (= We've been here from August to now.)

Circle the correct word.

1. I bought my car almost 10 years ago. I've had it **for / since** almost 10 years.
2. The Carters moved to Seattle six months ago. They've lived there **for / since** six months.
3. I've wanted to see that movie **for / since** a long time. It's been in theaters **for / since** March.

Unit 11

1 Adverbs before adjectives (page 73)

> ▶ Use *a/an* with (adverb) + adjective + singular noun: It's a **very modern city**.
> It's **an expensive city**. Don't use *a/an* with (adverb) + adjective:
> It's **really interesting**. (NOT: ~~It's a really interesting.~~)

Read the sentences. Add *a* or *an* where it's necessary to complete the sentences.

1. Brasília is extremely modern city.
   an
   ^

2. Seoul is very interesting place.

3. Santiago is pretty exciting city to visit.

4. Montreal is beautiful city, and it's fairly old.

5. London has really busy airport.

2 Conjunctions (page 74)

> ▶ Use *and* for additional information: The food is delicious, **and** it's not expensive.
> ▶ Use *but, though*, and *however* for contrasting information: The food is delicious, **but**
> it's very expensive. / The food is delicious. It's expensive, **though/however**.

Circle the correct word.

1. Spring in my city is pretty nice, **and / but** it gets extremely hot in summer.
2. There are some great museums. They're always crowded, **and / however**.
3. There are a lot of interesting stores, **and / but** many of them aren't expensive.
4. There are many amazing restaurants, **and / but** some are closed in August.
5. My city is a great place to visit. Don't come in summer **but / though**!

3 Modal verbs *can* and *should* (page 75)

> ▶ Use *can* to talk about things that are possible: Where **can** I get some nice souvenirs?
> Use *should* to suggest things that are good to do: You **should** try the local
> restaurants.
> ▶ Use the base form with *can* and *should* – not the infinitive: Where **can** I ~~to~~ get some
> nice souvenirs? You **should** ~~to~~ try the local restaurants.

Complete the conversation with *can, can't, should*, or *shouldn't*.

A: I ....*can't*........ decide where to go on vacation. .... I go to Costa Rica
   or Hawaii?
B: You .... definitely visit Costa Rica.
A: Really? What can I see there?
B: Well, San Jose is an exciting city. You .... miss the Museo del Oro. That's
   the gold museum, and you .... see beautiful animals made of gold.
A: OK. What else?
B: Well, you .... visit the museum on Mondays. It's closed then. But you
   .... definitely visit the rain forest. It's amazing!

Unit 12

1 Adjective + infinitive; infinitive + noun (page 79)

> ▶ In negative statements, *not* comes before the infinitive: With a cold, it's important **not to exercise** too hard. (NOT: ~~With a cold, it's important **to not exercise** too hard.~~)

Rewrite the sentences using the words in parentheses. Add *not* when necessary.

1. For a bad headache, you should relax and close your eyes. (a good idea)
   It's a good idea to relax and close your eyes when you have a headache.
2. You should put some cold tea on that sunburn. (sometimes helpful)
   ....
3. For a fever, you should take some aspirin. (important)
   ....
4. For a cough, you shouldn't drink milk. (important)
   ....
5. For sore muscles, you should take a hot bath. (sometimes helpful)
   ....
6. When you feel stressed, you shouldn't drink a lot of coffee. (a good idea)
   ....

2 Modal verbs *can, could, may* for requests; suggestions (page 81)

> ▶ In requests, *can, could,* and *may* have the same meaning. *May* is a little more formal than *can* and *could.*

Number the lines of the conversation. Then write the conversation below.

.... Yes, please. What do you suggest for itchy skin?
.... Here you are. Can I help you with anything else?
.... Sure I can. You should see a dentist!
...1... Hello. May I help you?
.... You should try this lotion.
.... Yes. Can you suggest something for a toothache?
.... OK. And could I have a bottle of aspirin?

A: Hello. May I help you? ....
B: ....
A: ....
B: ....
A: ....
B: ....
A: ....

Unit 13

1 *So, too, neither, either* (page 87)

> ▶ Use *so* or *too* after an affirmative statement: I'm crazy about sushi. **So am I./I am, too.**
>
> ▶ Use *neither* or *not either* after a negative statement: I don't like fast food. **Neither do I./I don't either.**
>
> ▶ With *so* and *neither*, the verb comes before the subject: **So am I.** (NOT: ~~So I am.~~) **Neither do I.** (NOT: ~~Neither I do.~~)

A Choose the correct response to show that B agrees with A.

1. A: I'm in the mood for something salty.
   B: (I am, too.)/ I do, too.
2. A: I can't stand fast food.
   B: **Neither do I. / I can't either.**
3. A: I really like Korean food.
   B: **So do I. / I am, too.**
4. A: I don't eat Italian food very often.
   B: **I do, too. / I don't either.**
5. A: I'm not crazy about pizza.
   B: **I am, too. / Neither am I.**

B Write responses to show agreement with these statements.

1. A: I'm not a very good cook.
   B: ....
2. A: I love french fries.
   B: ....
3. A: I can't eat very spicy food.
   B: ....
4. A: I never eat bland food.
   B: ....
5. A: I can make delicious desserts.
   B: ....

2 Modal verbs *would* and *will* for requests (page 89)

> ▶ Don't confuse *like* and *would like*. *Would like* means "want."
>
> ▶ You can also use *I'll have . . .* when ordering in a restaurant to mean *I will have . . . .*

Complete the conversation with *would, I'd,* or *I'll.*

A: <u>Would</u> you like to order now?
B: Yes, please. .... have the shrimp curry.
A: .... you like noodles or rice with that?
B: Hmm, ... have rice.
A: And .... you like a salad, too?
B: No, thanks.
A: .... you like anything else?
B: Yes, ... like a cup of green tea.

Unit 14

1 Comparisons with adjectives (page 93)

> ▶ Use the comparative form (adjective + -er or more + adjective) to compare two people, places, or things: Which river is **longer**, the Nile or the Amazon? The Nile is **longer than** the Amazon. Use the superlative form (the + adjective + -est or the most + adjective) to compare three or more people, places, or things: Which river is **the longest**: the Nile, the Amazon, or the Mississippi? The Nile is **the longest** river in the world.
> ▶ You can use a comparative or superlative without repeating the noun: Which country is **larger**, Canada or China? Canada is **larger**. What's the highest waterfall in the world? Angel Falls is **the highest**.

Write questions with the words. Then look at the underlined words, and write the answers.

1. Which desert / dry / the Sahara or <u>the Atacama</u>?
   Q: <u>Which desert is drier, the Sahara or the Atacama?</u>
   A: <u>The Atacama is drier than the Sahara.</u>
2. Which island / large / <u>Greenland</u>, New Guinea, or Honshu?
   Q: ....
   A: ....
3. Which island / small / New Guinea or <u>Honshu</u>?
   Q: ....
   A: ....
4. Which U.S. city / large / Los Angeles, Chicago, or <u>New York</u>?
   Q: ....
   A: ....
5. Who / older / your father or your <u>grandfather</u>?
   Q: ....
   A: ....

2 Questions with *how* (page 96)

> ▶ Use *high* to describe mountains and waterfalls: How **high** is Mount Fuji? Angel Falls is 979 meters **high**. Use *tall* to describe buildings: How **tall** is the Empire State Building? (NOT: ~~How high is the Empire State Building?~~)

Complete the questions with the phrases in the box. There is one extra phrase.

How big	How cold	✓ How deep	How high	How tall

1. Q: <u>How deep</u> is Lake Baikal?   A: It's 1,642 meters (5,387 feet) at its deepest point.
2. Q: .... is Alaska?   A: It's 586,412 square miles (1,518,800 kilometers).
3. Q: .... is Mount McKinley?   A: It's 20,300 feet (6,194 meters) high.
4. Q: .... is the CN Tower?   A: It is 553 meters (1,814 feet) tall.

Unit 15

1 Future with present continuous and *be going to* (page 101)

> ▶ Use the present continuous to talk about something that is happening now:
> What **are** you **doing**? I**'m studying.** You can also use the present continuous
> with time expressions to talk about the future: What **are** you **doing tomorrow**?
> I**'m working.**

A Read the sentences. Are they present or future? Write P or F.

1. Why are you wearing shorts? It's cold. ....P....
2. What are you wearing to the party on Friday? ....
3. Where are you going this weekend? ....
4. Where are you going? ....
5. Are you going to watch TV tonight? ....

B Complete the conversations. Use the present continuous and *be going to.*

1. A: What ....are........... you and Tony ....doing........ (do) tonight?
   B: We .... (try) the new Chinese restaurant. Would you like to come?
   A: I'd love to. What time .... you .... (go)?
   B: We .... (meet) at Tony's house at 7:00. And don't forget an umbrella.
      It .... (rain) tonight.
2. A: Where .... you .... (go) on vacation this year?
   B: I .... (visit) my cousins in Paris. It .... (be) great!
   A: Well, I .... (not go) anywhere this year. I .... (stay) home.
   B: That's not so bad. Just think about all the money you .... (save)!

2 Messages with *tell* and *ask* (page 103)

> ▶ In messages with a request, use the infinitive of the verb: Please ask her **to meet** me
> at noon. (NOT: ~~Please ask her meet me at noon.~~)
> ▶ In messages with negative infinitives, *not* goes before to in the infinitive: Could you
> ask him **not to be** late? (NOT: ~~Could you ask him to not be late?~~)

Read the messages. Ask someone to pass them on. Use the words in parentheses.

1. Message: Patrick – We don't have class tomorrow. (please)
   Please tell Patrick that we don't have class tomorrow.
2. Message: Ana – Call me tonight on my cell phone. (would)
   ....
3. Message: Alex – The concert on Saturday is canceled. (would)
   ....
4. Message: Sarah – Don't forget to return the book to the library. (could)
   ....

Unit 16

1 Describing change (page 107)

▶ You can use several tenses to describe change – present tense, past tense, and present perfect.

A Complete the sentences with the information in the box. Use the present perfect of the verbs given.

| buy a house | change her hairstyle | join a gym | start looking for a new job |

1. Pedro and Debbie .... Their apartment was too small.
2. Allen .... The one he has now is too stressful.
3. Sandra .... Everyone says it's more stylish.
4. Kevin .... He feels healthier now.

B Rewrite the sentences using the present tense and the words in parentheses.

1. Joy doesn't wear jeans anymore. *She wears dresses* .... (dresses)
2. They don't live in the city anymore. .... (suburbs)
3. Carol isn't shy anymore. .... (outgoing)
4. I quit eating greasy food. .... (healthier)

2 Verb + infinitive (page 109)

▶ Use the infinitive after a verb to describe future plans or things you want to happen: I **want to learn** Spanish.

Complete the conversation with the words in parentheses and a verb from the box. You can use some verbs more than once.

| be | do | drive | go | live | make | stay | work |

A: Hey, Steven. What ....*are you going to do*.... (go) after graduation?
B: Well, I .... (plan) here in the city for a few months.
A: Really? I .... (want) home. I'm ready for my mom's cooking.
B: I understand that, but my boss says I can keep my job for the summer. So I .... (want) a lot of hours because I .... (hope) enough money for a new car.
A: But you don't need a car in the city.
B: I .... (not plan) here for very long. In the fall, I .... (go) across the country. I really .... (want) in California.
A: California? Where in California .... (like)?
B: In Hollywood, of course. I .... (go) a movie star!

Grammar plus answer key

Unit 1

1 Statements with *be*; possessive adjectives

1. This **is** Delia Rios. **She's** a new student from Peru.
2. My name **is** Sergio. **I'm** from Brazil.
3. My brother and I **are** students here. **Our** names are Dave and Jeff.
4. **He's** Yoshi. **He's** 19 years old.
5. **They're** in my English class. **It's** a very big class.

2 Wh-questions with *be*

1. f
2. e
3. a
4. b
5. c
6. d

3 Yes/No questions and short answers with *be*

1. B: No, **they're not / they aren't**. They're in English 2.
2. A: Hi! **Are you** in this class?
   B: Yes, **I am**. I'm a new student here.
3. A: **Are you** from the United States?
   B: No, **we're not / we aren't**. We're from Montreal, Canada.
4. A: Hi, Sonia. **Are you** free?
   B: No, **I'm not**. I'm on my way to class.
5. A: That's the new student. **Is he** from Puerto Rico?
   B: No, **he's not / he isn't**. he's from Costa Rica.
6. A: **Is she** from Thailand?
   B: Yes, **she is**. She's from Bangkok.

Unit 2

1 Simple present Wh-questions and statements

1. A: I **have** good news! Dani **has** a new job.
   B: How **does** she **like** it?
   A: She **loves** it. The hours are great.
   B: What time **does** she **start**?
   A: She **starts** at nine and **finishes** at five.
2. A: What **do** you **do**?
   B: I'm a teacher.
   A: What **do** you **teach**?
   B: I **teach** Spanish, and English.
   A: Really? My sister **teaches** English, too.

2 Time expressions

B: I love it, but the hours are difficult. I start work **at** 7:30 A.M., and I work **until** 3:30.
A: That's interesting! I work the same hours, but I work **at** night. I start **at** 7:30 **in** the evening and finish **at** 3:30 **in** the morning.
B: Wow! What time do you get up?
A: Well, I get home **at** 4:30 and go to bed **at** 5:30. And I sleep **until** 2:00. But I only work **on** weekends, so it's OK. What about you?
B: Oh, I work **on** Monday, Wednesday, and Friday. And I get up **early** – around 6:00 A.M.

Unit 3

1 Demonstratives; *one, ones*

1. A: Excuse me. How much are **these** shoes?
   B: **They're** $279.
   A: And how much is **that** bag over there?
   B: **It's** only $129.
   A: And are the two gray **ones** $129, too?
   B: No. **Those** are only $119.
   A: Oh! **This** store is really expensive.
2. A: Can I help you?
   B: Yes, please. I really like **those** jeans over there. How much **are they**?
   A: Which **ones**? Do you mean **these**?
   B: No, the black **ones**.
   A: Let me look. Oh, **they're** $35.99.
   B: That's not bad. And how much is **this** sweater here?
   A: **It's** only $9.99.

2 Preferences; comparisons with adjectives

A

2. more boring
3. more exciting
4. friendlier
5. more interesting
6. more reasonable
7. sadder
8. warmer

B

2. I like the silver one (better). It's more interesting.
3. I prefer the silk one. It's prettier.
4. I like the purple ones (more). They're more exciting.

Unit 4

1 Simple present questions; short answers

A

2. A: **Does Joe like** Taylor Swift?
   B: No, **he doesn't**.
3. A: **Does Lisa like** talk shows?
   B: Yes, **she does**.
4. A: **Do you / you and Bob watch** the news on TV?
   B: Yes, **we do**.
5. A: **Do you like** hip-hop?
   B: No, **I don't**.
6. A: **Do your parents listen to** jazz?
   B: No, **they don't**.

B

2. us   3. them   4. him   5. her

2 *Would*; verb + *to* + verb

A: Would you like to see a movie with me tonight?
B: Yes, I would. What would you like to see?
A: I'd like to see the new Halle Berry movie.

Unit 5

1 Present continuous

1. A: **Is she living abroad?**
   B: Yes, **she is**. She**'s living / is living** in South Korea.
2. A: **How are you spending your summer?**
   B: I**'m working** part-time. I**'m taking** two classes also.
   A: **What are you taking?**
   B: My friend and I **are studying** photography and Japanese. We like our classes a lot.

2 Quantifiers

2. Nearly all students finish high school.
3. All children start school by the age of six.
4. A lot of couples have more than one child.
5. Few families have more than four children.

Unit 6

1 Adverbs of frequency

1. A: **I often play sports.**
2. Q: **Do you ever go jogging with a friend?**
   A: No, **I always jog / go jogging alone.**
3. Q: **How often do you play tennis?**
   A: **I play four times a week.**
4. Q: **What do you usually do in the evening?**
   A: My family and I almost always watch TV.
5. Q: **How often do you go to the gym?**
   A: **I never go (to the gym).**

2 Questions with *how*; short answers

1. **How often** do you lift weights? c
2. **How well** do you play tennis? a
3. **How good** are you at aerobics? d
4. **How long** do you spend at the gym? b

Unit 7

1 Simple past

B: Yes, I **did**. I **had** a great time. My sister and I **went** shopping on Saturday. We **spent** all day at the mall.
A: **Did** you **buy** anything special?
B: I **bought** a new laptop. And I **got** some new clothes, too.
A: Lucky you! What clothes **did** you **buy?**
B: Well, I **needed** some new boots. I **found** some great ones at Luff's Department Store.
A: What about you? What **did** you **do** on Saturday?
B: I **didn't do** anything special. I **stayed** home and **worked** around the house. Oh, but I **saw** a really good movie on TV. And then I **made** dinner with my mother. I actually **enjoyed** the day.

2 Past of *be*

2. He was at work all day.
3. Tony and his co-workers were at work on Saturday, too.
4. They weren't at work on Sunday.
5. Was Tony at home on Sunday?
6. Where was Tony on Sunday?
7. He and his brother were at a baseball game.
8. They were at the park until 7:00.

Unit 8

1 There is, there are; one, any, some

1. A: **Are** there any supermarkets in this neighborhood?
   B: No, there **aren't**, but there are **some** on Main Street.
   A: And **is** there a post office near here?
   B: Yes, **there is**. It's across from the bank.
2. A: **Is** there a gas station around here?
   B: Yes, **there's** one behind the shopping center.
   A: Great! And are there **any** coffee shops nearby?
   B: Yes, there's a good **one** in the shopping center.

2 Quantifiers; *how many* and *how much*

A

1. A: much
   B: a little
2. A: many
   B: many
3. A: How many
   B: are
4. A: How much
   B: none

B

2. A: Are there many parks?
3. A: Is there much crime?
4. A: Are there many laundromats?

Unit 9

1 Describing people

A: How tall is he?
B: He's 5 feet 11.
A: Does he wear glasses?
B: No, he doesn't. He wears contact lenses.
A: What color is his hair?
B: He has blond hair.
A: Does he have blue eyes?
B: No, he has brown eyes.
A: And how old is he?
B: He's 26 – two years older than me.

2 Modifiers with participles and prepositions

1. B: She's the one wearing a red dress.
2. A: Which ones are your neighbors?
   B: They're the ones walking with the baby.
3. A: Which one is Jeff?
   B: He's the one with glasses.

Unit 10

1 Present perfect; *already, yet*

A

2. B: No, she **hasn't called** me, but I**'ve gotten** some emails from her.
3. A: **Have** you and Jan **had** lunch yet?
   B: No, we **haven't**. We're thinking of going to Tony's. **Have** you **tried** it yet? Come with us.
   A: Thanks. I **haven't eaten** there yet, but I**'ve heard** it's pretty good.

B

2. I've **already** gone shopping.
3. Have you been to the zoo **yet**?
4. I've **already** talked to them./I've talked to them **already**.

2 Present perfect vs. simple past

1. A: **Did** you **see** the game last night? I really **enjoyed** it.
   B: Yes, I **did**. It **was** an amazing game. **Have** you ever **gone** to a game?
   A: No, I **haven't**. I've never **been** to the stadium. But I'd love to go! Maybe we can go to a game next year.
2. A: **Have** you ever **been** to Franco's Restaurant?
   B: Yes, I **have**. My friend and I **ate** there last weekend. How about you?
   A: No, I **haven't**. But I've **heard** it's very good.
   B: Oh, yes – it's excellent!

3 *For* and *since*

1. I've had it **for** almost 10 years.
2. They've lived there **for** six months.
3. I've wanted to see that movie **for** a long time. It's been in theaters **since** March.

Unit 11

1 Adverbs before adjectives

2. Seoul is **a** very interesting place.
3. Santiago is **a** pretty exciting city to visit.
4. Montreal is **a** beautiful city, and it's fairly old.
5. London has **a** really busy airport.

2 Conjunctions

1. Spring in my city is pretty nice, **but** it gets extremely hot in summer.
2. They're often crowded, **however**.
3. There are a lot of interesting stores, **and** many of them aren't expensive.
4. There are many amazing restaurants, **but** some are closed in August.
5. Don't come in summer, **though**!

3 Modal verbs *can* and *should*

A: I **can't** decide where to go on vacation. **Should** I go to Costa Rica or Hawaii?
B: You **should** definitely visit Costa Rica.
A: Really? What can I see there?
B: Well, San Jose is an exciting city. You **shouldn't** miss the Museo del Oro. That's the gold museum, and you **can** see beautiful animals made of gold.
A: OK. What else **can** I do there?
B: Well, you **can't** visit the museum on Mondays. It's closed then. But you **should** definitely visit the rain forest.

Unit 12

1 Adjective + infinitive; infinitive + noun

2. For a sunburn, **it's sometimes helpful to put** some cold tea on it.
3. For a fever, **it's important to take** some aspirin.
4. For a cough, **it's important not to drink** milk.
5. For sore muscles, **it's sometimes helpful to take** a hot bath.
6. When you feel stressed, **it's not a good idea to drink** a lot of coffee.

2 Modal verbs *can, could, may* for requests; suggestions

2. Yes, please. What do you suggest for itchy skin?
3. You should try this lotion.
4. OK. And could I have a bottle of aspirin?
5. Here you are. Can I help you with anything else?
6. Yes. Can you suggest something for a toothache?
7. Sure I can. You should see a dentist!

Unit 13

1 *So, too, neither, either*

A

2. B: I can't either.
3. B: So do I.
4. B: I don't either.
5. B: Neither am I.

B

1. B: I'm not either.
2. B: I do, too.
3. B: I can't either.
4. B: Neither do I.
5. B: So can I.

2 Modal verbs *would* and *will* for requests

B: I'll
A: Would
B: I'll
A: would
A: Would
B: I'd

Unit 14

1 Comparisons with adjectives

2. Q: Which island is the largest: Greenland, New Guinea, or Honshu?
   A: Greenland is the largest.
3. Q: Which island is smaller, New Guinea or Honshu?
   A: Honshu is smaller than New Guinea.
4. Q: Which U.S. city is the largest: Los Angeles, Chicago, or New York?
   A: New York is the largest.
5. Q: Who is older, your father or your grandfather?
   A: Your / My grandfather is older.

2 Questions with *how*

2. How big
3. How high
4. How tall

Unit 15

1 Future with present continuous and *be going to*

A

2. F
3. F
4. P
5. F

B

1. B: We **we're going to try** the new Chinese restaurant. Would you like to come?
   A: I'd love to. What time **are** you are **you going to go**?
   B: We**'re going to meet** at Tony's house at 7:00. And don't forget an umbrella. It**'s going to rain** tonight.
2. A: Where **are** you **going to go** on vacation this year?
   B: I**'m going to visit** my cousins in Paris. It**'s going to be** great!
   A: Well, I**'m not going to go** anywhere this year. I**'m going to stay** home.
   B: That's not so bad. Just think about all the money you**'re going to save!**

2 Messages with *tell* and *ask*

2. Would you ask Ana to call me tonight on my cell phone?
3. Would you tell Alex (that) the concert on Saturday is canceled?
4. Could you tell Sarah not to forget to return the book to the library?

Unit 16

1 Describing change

A

1. Pedro and Debbie **have bought a house**.
2. Allen **has started looking for a new job**.
3. Sandra **has changed her hairstyle**.
4. Kevin **has joined a gym**.

B

Possible answers:

2. They live in the suburbs.
3. Carol / She is outgoing.
4. I eat healthier now.

2 Verb + infinitive

B: Well, I **plan to stay** here in the city for a few months.
A: Really? I **want to go** home. I'm ready for my mom's cooking.
B: I understand that, but my boss says I can keep my job for the summer. So I **want to work** a lot of hours because I **hope to make** enough money for a new car.
A: But you don't need a car in the city.
B: I **don't plan to be** here for very long. In the fall, I'm **going to drive** across the country. I really **want to live** in California.
A: California? Where in California **would you like to live**?
B: In Hollywood, of course. I**'m going to be** a movie star!

Credits

Illustrations

Andrezzinho: 32, 60, 120; **Ilias Arahovitis:** 17 (*bottom center, right*), 117, 126; **Ralph Butler:** 88, 102; **Mark Collins:** v; **Paul Daviz:** 33, 59, 90 (*top*); **Rob De Bank:** 17 (*center*), 42; **Carlos Diaz:** 127; **Tim Foley:** 17 (*bottom left*); **Travis Foster:** 14, 68, 71; **Chuck Gonzales:** 11, 16 (*bottom*), 37, 100 (*bottom*); **Jim Haynes:** 19, 25 (*bottom*), 93, 106; **Dan Hubig:** 17 (*top*), 18, 40; **Randy Jones:** 9, 39, 44, 85, 86 (*bottom*), 91, 108, 110, 116, 117; **Trevor Keen:** 25 (*top*), 53 (*top*), 58, 100 (*top*); **Joanna Kerr:** 50 (*top*), 80, 121

Kja-artists: 4, 70, 107; **Eric Larsen:** 115; **Shelton Leong:** 2, 3, 5, 129; **Monika Melnychuk:** 20; **Karen Minot:** 16 (*top*), 51, 55, 92; **Rob Schuster:** 28, 36 (*bottom*), 77, 86 (*top*), 100 (*top*), 105, 122, 128; **Daniel Vasconcellos:** 78 (*top*), 113, 131; **Brad Walker:** 50 (*bottom*), 61 (*bottom*), 81; **Sam Whitehead:** 31, 53 (*bottom*), 64 (*bottom*), 66, 67, 78 (*bottom*), 79, 114; **James Yamasaki:** 30, 47, 56, 103, 123, 124; **Rose Zgodzinski:** 36 (*top*), 38, 74, 96, 111, 125; **Carol Zuber-Mallison:** 61(*top*), 69, 83, 89, 97, 118

Photos

6 (*top to bottom*) © Echo/Cultura/Getty Images; © Hemera/Thinkstock
7 © Jill Fromer/iStockphoto
8 (*clockwise from top left*) © Rich Legg/iStockphoto; © Zhang Bo/iStockphoto; © AP Photo/Phil Sandlin; © Jose Luis Pelaez Inc/Blend Images; © Fuse/Getty Images; © Radius Images/Alamy
9 (*left to right*) © Glowimages RM/Alamy; © Rudyanto Wijaya/iStockphoto; © Joe Belanger/Shutterstock; © West Coast Surfer/Moodboard/Age Fotostock; © Jeff Greenberg/Alamy; © Jose Luis Pelaez Inc./Blend Images
10 (*top to bottom*) © Tetra Images/Alamy; © Ariel Skelley/Blend Images
11 © Yellow Dog Productions/Lifesize/Getty Images
12 (*top to bottom*) © Duard van der Westhuizen/Shutterstock; © Purestock/Getty Images
13 (*all*) (Eddie Chen) © Red Chopsticks/Getty Images; (Julia Brown) © Andrew Rich/iStockphoto; (Denise Parker) © Roberto Westbrook/Blend Images/Getty Images
15 (*top, left to right*) © Digital Vision/Thinkstock; © Kent Meireis/The Image Works; © Lothar Wels/Masterfile; © LWA/Dann Tardif/Blend Images/Getty Images; (*bottom*) © iStockphoto/Thinkstock
19 (*top, left to right*) © Terex/Fotolia; © Hemera/Thinkstock; © Hemera Technologies/AbleStock.com/Thinkstock; © largeformat4x5/iStockphoto; (*middle, left to right*) © Gary Alvis/iStockphoto; © Vedius/Alamy; © Stockbyte/Thinkstock; © Terex/iStockphoto
21 (*top right*) © Sean Locke/iStockphoto; (*middle, left*) © Leaf/Veer
23 (*top to bottom*) © Jemal Countess/Getty Images; © m78/ZUMA Press/Newscom; © AP Photo/Paul Drinkwater
24 (*middle, left to right*) © Sthanlee B. Mirador Pacific Rim/Newscom; © Jeffrey R. Staab/CBS Photo Archive/Getty Images; (*bottom, left to right*) © FRANCK FIFE/AFP/Getty Images; © g90/ZUMA Press/Newscom
27 (*top to bottom*) © Paul Gilham/FIFA/Getty Images; © MGM/Courtesy Everett Collection; © Ronald Martinez/Getty Images
28 (*all*) (wool pants) © Gordana Sermek/Shutterstock; (silk shirt) © PhotoObjects.net/Thinkstock; (laptop, desktop, cotton shirt) © iStockphoto/Thinkstock
29 © Robert Holmes/Corbis
31 (*all*) (Chris Martin) © Steve Granitz/WireImage/Getty Images; (Francis Ford Coppola) © Steve Mack/WireImage/Getty Images; (Miley Cyrus) © Steve Granitz/WireImage/Getty Images; (Casey Affleck) © Kurt Krieger/Corbis; (Gwyneth Paltrow) © Steve Granitz/WireImage/Getty Images; (Nicholas Cage) © Pier Giorgio Brunelli/FilmMagic/Getty Images; (Billy Ray Cyrus) © Steve Granitz/WireImage/Getty Images; (Jennifer Garner) © Nancy Kaszerman/ZUMA Press/Corbis
34 (*top to bottom*) © Lane Oatey/Getty Images; © iStockphoto/Thinkstock; © Westend61/SuperStock
35 (*clockwise from left*) © Jose Luis Pelaez Inc/Blend Images; © Juice Images/Cultura/Getty Images; © BananaStock/Thinkstock
37 © Jupiterimages/Brand X Pictures/Thinkstock
38 (*left to right*) © Mango Productions/Comet/Corbis; © Goodshoot/Thinkstock; © Ilja Mašík/Shutterstock; © Tetra Images/Alamy; © Ale Ventura/PhotoAlto/Photolibrary
39 (*left to right*) © Ben Queenborough/BPI/Corbis; © Robert Cianflone/Getty Images
40 © DiMaggio/Kalish/Corbis
43 © Ocean/Corbis
44 (*top, left to right*) © imagebroker/Alamy; © iStockphoto/Thinkstock; © Imagesource/Photolibrary; © Filaphoto/Shutterstock; (*middle, left to right*) © Skip ODonnell/iStockphoto; © Martin Moxter/Photolibrary; © Arctic-Images/Alamy; © James Steidl/iStockphoto
46 © Sean Cayton/The Image Works
47 © Manamana/Shutterstock
48 © iStockphoto/Thinkstock
49 (*top to bottom*) © Tibor Bognár/Age Fotostock; © IanDagnall/Alamy; © blickwinkel/Alamy
52 © Dennis MacDonald/Age Fotostock

54 © Tim Graham/Getty Images
55 © Jean Heguy/First Light/Alamy
60 © Comstock/Thinkstock
61 (*top, left to right*) © Hemera/Thinkstock; © Koki Iino/Getty Images; © Ryan McVay/Stone/Getty Images
63 (*top, right*) © Jupiterimages/Thinkstock; (*middle, top to bottom*) © Stefan Gosatti/Getty Images; © Francois Guillot/AFP/Getty Images; © Rudy k/Alamy
64 (*top, left to right*) © Franz Marc Frei/Look/Age Fotostock; © John Elk III/Alamy; © Jim West/Age Fotostock; © Antonella Carri/Marka/Age Fotostock; © Wendy Kaveney/Danita Delimont/Alamy
69 (*clockwise from top*) © Scholz/Mauritius Images/Age Fotostock; © Andrew Peacock/Getty Images; © Chappuis Blaise/Rapsodia/Age Fotostock
72 (*top to bottom*) © Gerth Roland/Age Fotostock; © Nik Wheeler/Corbis; © Walter Bibikow/Age Fotostock
73 © Mark L Stephenson/Surf/Corbis
74 (*middle*) © John Coletti/JAI/Corbis; (*bottom, clockwise from left*) © Katja Kreder/Imagebroker/Alamy; © Joel Saget/AFP/Getty Images; © R Sigaev/Zoonar/Age Fotostock; © Supri/RTR/Newscom; © Florian Kopp/imagebroker/Age Fotostock; © Hermes Images/Tips Images RM/Age Fotostock
75 © Frilet Patrick/Hemis/Alamy
76 (*top*) © EckPhoto/Alamy; (*bottom*) © Philippe Michel/Age Fotostock/Photolibrary
77 (*top to bottom*) © Timothy Allen/Axiom Photographic Agency/Getty Images; © Greg Johnston/Danita Delimont/Alamy; © Chris Caldicott/Axiom Photographic Agency/Age Fotostock
80 © Brand X Pictures/Thinkstock
81 © Beauty Photo Studio/Age Fotostock
82 © Bill Ling/Digital Vision/Getty Images
83 (*top, right*) © Thornton Cohen/Alamy; (*middle*) © John Glover/Alamy
86 (*top, left to right*) © Esbin-Anderson/Age Fotostock; © Hamza Türkkol/iStockphoto; © iStockphoto/Thinkstock; © Bronze Photography/Healthy Food Images/Age Fotostock; (*middle, left to right*) © Iryna Dobrovyns'ka/iStockphoto; © iStockphoto/Thinkstock; © Dino Osmic/iStockphoto; © ALEAIMAGE/iStockphoto
87 (*middle, clockwise from left*) (healthy, delicious, rich) © iStockphoto/Thinkstock; © Polka Dot/Thinkstock; © Vikif/iStockphoto; © Hemera/Thinkstock; © Digital Vision/Thinkstock
89 © foodfolio/Alamy
90 © Jose Luis Pelaez, Inc./Corbis
94 (*middle, left to right*) © Shelly Perry/iStockphoto; © iStockphoto/Thinkstock; © Photos.com/Thinkstock
95 © Robert Harding/Digital Vision/Getty Images
96 © TongRo Image Stock/Alamy
97 (*top, left to right*) © Comstock/Thinkstock; © Kim Karpeles/Alamy; © iStockphoto/Thinkstock; © Dian Lofton; (*middle, left to right*) © iStockphoto/Thinkstock; © Joy Brown/Shutterstock; © Andre Blais/Shutterstock; © Trista/Shutterstock
99 © Classic Vision/Age Fotostock
102 © Daniel Boczarski/Getty Images
109 (*middle, top to bottom*) © Image Source/Alamy; © Creatas/Thinkstock; © Blend Images/Getty Images
112 © Craig Ferguson/Alamy
118 (*middle, clockwise from left*) © David Lyons/Alamy; © Jeff Greenberg/Age Fotostock; © Valerie Armstrong/Alamy; © Javier Pierini/Stone/Getty Images
119 (*top, left to right*) © DreamPictures/Blend Images; © Jack Hollingsworth/Digital Vision/Thinkstock; © Todd Warnock/Lifesize/Thinkstock
130 (*bottom, left to right*) © David Leahy/Taxi/Getty Images; © Tokyo Feminine Styling/Getty Images; © Masterfile.